A PEOPLE'S PRIMER

DISPATCHES ON POLITICS AND SOCIAL CHANGE

Crystallee Crain

Kendall Hunt
publishing company

Cover image © Shutterstock.com

www.kendallhunt.com
Send all inquiries to:
4050 Westmark Drive
Dubuque, IA 52004-1840

Published in the United States of America

"Knowledge is power that catalyzes the fullest capacity of our humane and compassionate natures. Our quest for the truth can ignite our curiosity for change, joy and peace in the world."

DR CRYSTALLEE CRAIN

Table of Contents

Introduction

Politics is about the distribution of resources. Resources as in products, nature, and in some aspects of our society, people are being bought and sold.

While we are sleeping and living our lives, the distribution of resources from a national central government trickles to the states and down to various municipalities. This process of complex governing bodies uses formulas to determine the exact numbers and how this process happens.

These tax dollars are meant to be returned to us in the form of programs, jobs, quality schools, health care, and other needs. What does this mean for you—an average person living and working to make ends meet? In our democracy, our written and implied social contract with the government says that by paying taxes, we are owed public services. These available services are supposed to alleviate the struggles of life, not to perpetuate them. Much of our tax money is spent in developing our community's infrastructure or the lack thereof. Infrastructure, like roads, the train system, and public utilities, are paid for, in large part, by our tax dollars. We are most familiar with the funding of our public school systems, the transit systems (buses and trains), and our library systems.

In other instances, the democratic distribution gets caught up in the way of our economic market that is shaped by capitalistic ideals. A Marxist view of our economic system identifies the workers as having a very distinct relationship from the owners. This is meant to explain the relations of production between classes of people and their relationship to the state or private entity.

The primary purpose of capitalism is to have the means of production privately owned. This type of ownership increases the power and control of wealth at the top while those without them, the workers, earn money to provide for basic needs. The interests of capitalism imply that the owners should pay their workers as little as possible to ensure higher profits. This makes a private corporation profitable in a capitalistic system. Within the United States, the labor movement from the 18th century until today is responsible for having a federal minimum wage, that depending on the region of the country—does not provide for all basic needs.

The irony is that one employee, in one day, could make more profit for their company as a cashier with a till that cashes out with $5,000 in sales and will make $90 that week for their paycheck. Economic challenges of inequality have consistently presented problems on all fronts of our governmental system. The promise of the American Dream does not sit well with people who literally worked as hard as they could and still find themselves suffering economically—hence socially, politically, and personally. The reality of this notion passed two generations ago when not having a college degree didn't automatically mean low wages.

Many people are caught in the battle between blame, shame, and entitlement. In our democracy, we have not yet learned how to properly respond to our own social suffering without blaming others. We actively working to dismantle another person's chance while falsely assuming that it will increase our own.

Some people do not believe that there is a necessity for family based assistance programs, yet they supported the bailout of the banks in 2008, which is considered corporate welfare. Support to individuals has a stigma of helping the undeserving poor vs. the deserving poor. This moral question keeps us as a nation-state divided on how to manage resources.

The misinterpretation of entitlement programs by our Congressional leaders who actively work to reduce the federally managed program called Social Security puts our future at risk. This safety net, which is paid for by the American people, is often characterized as a handout. Those in power rely on misinformation to mislead us to believe that entitlement programs mean anything besides what it says. We paid for it; we are entitled to it.

Public resources are funded by the people and subsidized by tax dollars through state and federal government programs from sales, estate, income tax, etc. When these tax dollars are used for public services, there is an implied and written notion of accountability. The distribution of power is unequal; therefore, our individual and group's ability to access basic needs are also not just. This also goes for the attention given and biased treatment of corporations over people. Corporations are able to remove individual and group liability based on the classification and often times financial resources to sway the meaning of that classification in their favor. This is different than the state, not all state agents have immunity. This is an example of how some of the American values are applied in real-time to maintain certain social and legal realities.

These are just a handful of the factors that guide the overall distribution of wealth.

In the capitalist western world, we see resources being defined by what can be bought, sold, and traded. Resources are rarely shared humanely (based on need) and those that are there for humanitarian causes are limited. People are born into this world without the choice of citizenship and any warning of the condition of their communities. We grow into adults and citizens of a nation that we did not yet create. Regardless of this fact, our personhood and ability to participate in the world equally is based on where you are born. The histories of our ancestors are carried with us in our genes and our behaviors define our socio-political environment.

Some believe that we have a responsibility to increase the quality of life for ourselves and everyone around us. In this book, I aim to share information and opportunities for engagement that can be utilized by educators, families, and other groups to dream of a time when we are all on the same page with unified action and purpose.

In the United States, the mainstream, often eurocentric, definitions of what shapes a reasonable and worthy quality of life is measured by our attachment to products and images of wealth. Everything from our personal relationships, our education, our travel, to what we are able to purchase or have to survive is regulated by an economic system that is sometimes regulated by our government. This system needs us to participate in order to work. It's working when we are active consumers.

As Rev. Dr Martin Luther King expressed that we, in the United States, are indebted to the rest of the world before we even leave our house each day. From King's, A Christmas Sermon of Peace (1967), we learn about the complexities our American lives rest in as it relates to the invisible exchanges of class-based connections across borders.

Globally we all play a role in the economic systems that define the structures of our lives. We are intricately connected, and our fates rely on each other's understanding of that impact and a definitive choice to live so others can co-exist beside you.

In this country, we do not have the most righteous people-centered apparatus to infuse our voices for social change. This is why we see people demonstrating and taking action at an unprecedented rate. Since the election of Donald Trump as President of the United States, we have seen our general desire to develop political agency increase across all communities. When Trump unveiled his first attempt at an Executive Order to ban Muslims from entering the country, thousands of people took to the streets and started filling up airports nationwide. This was a sign of an increased understanding of our political system and a deeper desire to stand for our neighbors.

When learning about a political system, we see Republicans and Democrats urging people to give the new President a chance as we enter the next four years of Trump's reign. We also see an increase in white supremacy groups in this country taking charge of their views and making public statements through news agencies like Breitbart News, Twitter, and anti-semitic attacks on Jewish burial sites.

When learning about a political system, it's important to be exposed to more than just the functional aspects of each branch and the laws and regulations that dictate a governing bodies practice; because what we've seen is that these rules do not always apply, especially when there is no one within the political structure to hold individuals and corporations accountable. With a public and private school system that promotes the highest levels of inequity, we are stricken with a political education that is dismal at best. So this knowledge and these facts are crucial at this stage in our education.

Chris Hedges (2015) said it[t] best in his article on TruthDig:

> "The elites, trained in business schools and managerial programs not to solve real problems but to maintain at any cost the systems of global capitalism, profit personally from the assault. They amass inconceivable sums of wealth while their victims, the underclasses around the globe, are thrust into increasing distress from global warming, poverty, and societal breakdown."

With over a decade of teaching in community colleges and universities, I've witnessed the damage done to people's ability to self-actualize as they enter a classroom. Their primary interest is in their public image and appearance and less interest in the survival of their culture, let alone the human race. This reduces many to groveling at the chance to obtain degrees of higher education in order to get a spot on the pecking order of our economic system. And others whose path out of poverty included higher education, the penalty for a lack of economic stability early on in life is paid through student loans that cripple their ability to thrive. Proper education is necessary for any democratically leaning nation to fully function. Proper, as in honestly removed from the colonial framework that so many believe to be an honest representation of how the United States of America came to be. Proper, as in accurate to what is necessary for whole-person development, not just actors in a capitalist economy.

Today, the effectiveness of the system's functioning has been dismantled life for millions as we know it. Our economic systems remove people from their homes and create the state of homelessness as a personal problem rather than a social failure.

© Holli/Shutterstock.com

Our environment is suffering at such a high rate that many speculate famine and water wars. As reported in *The Guardian*, Oliver Milman (2015) wrote that, "of nine worldwide processes that underpin life on Earth, four have exceeded "safe" levels—human-driven climate change, loss of biosphere integrity, land system change and the high level of phosphorus and nitrogen flowing into the oceans due to fertilizer use." This is a reality that many are not prepared to take on personally, economically or politically. How will we prepare our families for a natural disaster today? Who will be criminalized for trying to survive? Criminalized like the low-income communities and communities of color were after Hurricane Katrina (2005).

The way in which public, private, and natural resources are managed in our democracy are highly influenced by our culture of greed (masked as profit) and the political relationships we have with other nations around the world (foreign relations). These dynamics are not commonly known, and the information that is shared by mainstream media is skewed for silent participation in what is allowed without sharing information to engage and activate a global citizenry for change.

Joshua Keating (2014) reported in *Slate Magazine*, that "when NBC News Foreign Correspondent Ayman Mohyeldin was removed from Gaza shortly after reporting on the killing of four boys in an airstrike on a Gaza beach, he was reinstated four days later following a widespread social media backlash. Newspaper headlines downplaying Palestinian casualties have also been roundly criticized." Our relationship to nations, such as Israel, impact what we know about their conflicts and our role in perpetuating the militarization of international conflict with our economic power—i.e., consumption.

In this way, we can see that politics is very personal. There are few decisions we make in a day that is not predetermined on a list of options pre-made and managed by someone else. Depending on where you fall in the hierarchy of a particular system, your life chances vary. Social mobility is often sold with higher education. Even now, a college degree doesn't live up to its promise.

Regardless of class, we are all contributing to the violence forced upon others around the world with our tax dollars and general level of inaction. The United States has 5% of the world's population and we use over 40% of the world's resources. We believe that we have very little choice in that matter, but this is a level of mental slavery that allows complacency to come first before human responsibility. The less you know, some think, the better. I believe that if we knew what our tax dollars were paying for, we would have a different response to the state of things.

Why do we tolerate inequality around us? What long-term benefit do we have from participating in capitalism? It's been shown to be disastrous to our health and has been crippled many people to believe that their value as a human being is measured by their ability to attain capital. This is weakening our ability to defend ourselves in thought and in action.

Federally, we have struggled to maintain a system of "checks and balances" within three branches of government that in writing attempt to represent "citizens" of this country equally. There are a number of contradictions within the system that shows us how our divisive cultural elements seep throughout our country. In recent years, attention has been brought to the thousands if not millions of untested rape kits. Nationwide, practically every state has thousands of rape kits that have gone untested. For the victims and survivors of the heinous crime of rape—in order to get a rape kit takes effort and emotional strain to go through the process. Police departments across the United States have failed to protect women equally. Women who are the highest reported survivors of rape. Where is the oversight for this? District Attorneys, County Prosecutors, and leaders inside governmental institutions are stepping up to amend this stark misuse of tax dollars.

In 2009 Kym Worthy, Wayne County Prosecutor discovered approximately 11,341 untested rape kits that were collecting dust in an old Detroit Police Department building. According to End The BackLog, a program of the Joyful Heart Foundation, Detroit has seen progress in cases of sexual assault after taking on the untested kits.

End The BackLog reports that:

> "As of October 2015, Detroit has tested approximately 10,000 kits, resulting in 2,616 DNA matches and the identification of 652 potential serial rapists. The Wayne County Prosecutor's Office has obtained 27 convictions, and DNA from the kits tested linked to crimes committed in 39 states and Washington DC."

With this misstep of justice, we have survivors being called now 5 to 15 years after their sexual assault to ID their perpetrators fueling additional pain and disrupting these women's lives again. Is this what our constitution guarantees women under the "right to life, liberty and the pursuit of happiness?" Why hasn't this been a priority in this country if we have equal protection under the law?

The value of constitutional freedoms and rights granted and protected by the law rarely holds true for all people. Mainstream politics provides us with a new media industry that is highly sanctioned by advertising dollars. Providing a so-called Fair and Balanced report is often full of personal commentary from hosts and segments of fact laced with ideological twists. This has left many people living in the United States unsure of what direction to take politically and passive observers to each other's oppression. Although Obama spearheaded an initiative called My Brother's Keeper, an effort to bring light to the concerns for men and boys of color in the United States, we are still witnessing daily men of color being killed for mistaken identity, false arrests, and unjustifiable homicide. I urge us to ask ourselves— do we have the country, the space, the life that we know we deserve as human being. What are we willing to do in order to get it? How can we teach future generations that their success does not have to come on the backs of other people? When and how can we shift our secondary and postsecondary education to focus on developing global citizens who aim to thrive without profiting off the plight of other people.

I urge us to ask ourselves—do we have the country, the space, the life that we know we deserve as human being. What are we willing to do in order to get it? How can we teach future generations that their success does not have to come on the backs of other people? When and how can we shift our secondary and postsecondary education to focus on developing global citizens who aim to thrive without profiting off the plight of other people.

This book is dedicated to that vision. Re-written for public consumption, this book began as a textbook for my political science students. Thousands of students have had access to this content as an e-book. I regularly updated the content, sometimes each semester or when the world changes. This is my final edition of this type of book as I'm moving on to other projects. I share this with you as a gift and hopefully a tool. I would love to educators to use it, parents, youth groups, families, and concerned individuals trying to a faster and more honest introduction to our political system without the drum roll of apathy as the underlying and ignored current.

We need new tools to solve this century's most complex problems. We need to understand our collective struggle so we can reexamine and redesign our lives that promote the most just ways of being. This book is a contribution to that growing tool box. We, as in people who live in the United States, need a tool that acknowledges students as members of families and communities disparately impacted by unequal and unchecked systems. We need critical analysis not just for the sake of balance but to intentionally expose and remove power where it is being abused. I want my readers to feel inspired to uncover corruption and re-establish values that will promote living a just life and relying on self determination to heal our communities. My book promotes a vision of the reader's family and peer group(s) as their very own organizing base.

Ideologically this book presents a strong narrative concerning those directly removed, maimed, disenfranchised, and displaced by actors and others agents of the U.S. government. Unfortunately, these acts have been numerous, and the number of necessary and important narratives are too many to capture in one book. In the end, I focused on domestic concerns with relevant recent international realities that shape what we're facing today as a nation.

In this book, I unpack some of the dynamics behind our individual and group relationships to the state as the foundation for a critical active approach to global citizenry. I examine our structures through examples that are generally left of our traditional approaches to re-telling history and understanding of political philosophy. When readers finish my book, I hope that they have a greater understanding of who they are in relationship to other people. I hope that collectively we will know how our daily decisions impact our neighbors and the environment.

In 2020, the United Stated commemorated the 100 years since the 1920 ratified decision to remove barriers to women's access to the right to vote. While the constitutional amendment in 1920 was fought primarily by white women in the United States, aiming to gain the same level of political participation as white and black men. Congress passed the 19th amendment on June 4th, 1919, and it was ratified on August 18th, 1920.

While the protection of these rights was not officially legislated until the Civil Rights Act and the Voting Rights Act, we have found that our democracy relies on the belief that our society is ruled by the people for the people. In our so-called democracy, we sit uncomfortably on a line of inequality that is partially due to our consistent and compliant participation in our economic and political system. In order to maintain wealth and power, those in power must create incentives for us—the people—to act in ways that we believe is in our own best self-interest. In reality, what we do directly increases the power of others and reduces our individual and collective power to redesign and restructure our society.

The way in which we choose to participate in our society provides a level of consent or approval for the institutions and groups we are affiliated with intentionally and unintentionally. In politics, this is very important. Many students come to institutions of higher education looking for a specific outcome. This outcome comes in many forms: approval, a degree, a job, or a community of concern.

Some students come to college with an internal claim of self-congratulatory victory to have access to utilize the pay to play system of higher education to increase their likelihood of being at the top of the economic pecking order. Meaning—how far up the list of haves and haves not are you willing to live with? What sacrifices within this capitalist system are you willing to make—to make it? We are led to believe that we have masterful control over these circumstances.

Many people believe that their liberation is tied solely to their ability to obtain wealth by any means necessary. We are socially conditioned to respond to the stimuli regarding money and desirable material goods as a sign of high character or value in society. This is damaging to ourselves as individuals but as a democracy when our motivations are tied up into superficial human responses to power and powerlessness.

For example, for many college students, the goal of obtaining a degree is to make money. Rarely do we see people eager to learn outside of the economic constraint and necessity to compete in the workforce. This goal is notable, for we in the United States are hard-wired to participate in the "race to the top." We are told that if we go to school, get good grades, we will get the job and the American Dream life that is sold to us on television. For individuals like myself, higher education was a stepping stone toward social mobility. Social inclusion into the rooms and even at times seats at powerful decision making tables. Unfortunately, this social mobility does not guarantee equal protection under the law. This is not a part of the ads peddled by admission counselors.

Unfortunately for many people, even the means to provide food for themselves and their families are not guaranteed without a degree. Our economic system of capitalism forces people to continue to legitimize themselves in order to compete on the "job market." This is a 20th century cultural phenomena that is changing drastically in this new century. The changes we are seeing are due to the increase in college educated people, the rise of the Internet as a new "place" for enterprise and work, and the internationalization of the job market.

Because of this reality, many people rush through their education because they have an economic imperative, or they don't finish their education at all because they have to work.

This economic injustice creates an imbalance between those who are able to complete higher education and those who cannot. These circumstances, coupled with the increase in public university tuition costs, have increased the financial strain on students. Much of this financial strain is put off onto student loans. In California, the UC tuition rates have increased over 80% since the 1970s. This increase is far above the necessity to escalate costs to align with inflation. Our ability to obtain a just education shouldn't be attached to our access to monetary means. Capitalism forces us to participate in this system if we want to get a higher education. This forced participation molds us into people who learn to give consent to systems and processes that do not fully serve our best interest.

Most of us passively participate in the student loan opportunities without knowing the full risk. Consent to the student loan companies comes in the form of your signature and your individual financial need. Every time you sign, you're submitting yourself to the fine print and to the business practices of those loan companies. This level of consent happens in our personal lives, and this is what makes everything political.

CHAPTER ONE

Genocide, The American Experiment, and Colonial Ambitions

What is the American Experiment? Mainstream texts present the development of the American political system as a tale of religious persecution and righteous acts of nationalism in the name of freedom and equality.

Jillson (2013) writes that American Political Development (APD) is the study of "contemporary American political institutions or practices [that] is enriched and deepened by understanding their origins, as well as the changes and reforms they have undergone in arriving at their moderns forms" (p. 4).

In 1776, when the United States of America first officially sought independence from British colonial rule, there was hope that America would govern and facilitate resources differently from its former British counterparts. The Declaration of Independence (1776) and the Bill of Rights (1789) were written as a means to secure the protection of people through civil liberties. A major critique of these documents is that they did not include the rights of women, indigenous people, and other people that were not white male property owners. On paper, the United States was a great melting pot, with all citizens free to experience "Life, liberty, and the pursuit of happiness." Thus began the American Experiment. So at what point did immigration laws become more important than ensuring that all children receive a thorough education? When did offering tax breaks for defense contractors become more palatable than PTSD treatment for war veterans? As time progressed, more people started immigrating and settling in America, and it became difficult to track and respond to everyone's needs. The truth behind politics and government is that they always look reasonable on paper, and nothing would get done if the laws, amendments, and bills seem askew in any way to the real people in power.

© Becky Wright Photography/Shutterstock.com

Upon careful analysis it becomes starkly apparent that this new American independence was meant exclusively for property-owning, white men. When the Declaration of Independence was signed, people of African descent were considered only three-fifths human, and the indigenous people who originally welcomed the English settlers were later massacred in the pursuit of their land. Even white women did not win the right to vote until 1920, when the Nineteenth Amendment was passed after years of protest during the women's suffrage movement. Freedom in "the land of the free" has never been a guarantee.

In this context, it becomes clear that there is a flaw with the cultural ideal of the "American Dream." This false sense of guaranteed upward mobility and entitlement are strong within the social norms of what American's expect in their social and economic lives. The Civil War brought about the Emancipation Proclamation and the Thirteenth Amendment, which eradicated slavery. The worker rebellions at the turn of the 20th century paved the way for improved working conditions and the end of child labor. More recently, the brief Occupy Movement brought attention to the alarming income disparity and distribution of wealth in America, which benefits the entitled, wealthy class at the expense of the poor. The movement focused some much needed attention to the power dynamic which has been universally accepted as reality, and it encouraged citizens to question an economy that ultimately does not serve them. In each of these acts, there has been a demand for ideals that would eventually culminate into an "American Dream," one of independence, freedom, fair treatment, fair pay, and transparency. However, that American Dream, or the ideal American life, has often excluded the needs and desires of many groups of people. The 1950's version of the iconic nuclear family with the white picket fence was conceived with the standard white, heterosexual family in mind. There are strict socio-economic class, race, and gender requirements that must be satisfied before it is attainable. If those requirements are not satisfied to the letter, then there exists a stratosphere wherein the American Dream becomes the American nightmare that often goes unnoticed or is misrepresented through media, education, and political propaganda. The path to the American Dream is depicted in history books as bloody, but well-deserved. As such, it spreads the misconception that, because America has it better than other countries, that change is not only impossible, but unnecessary. In this chapter, we will discover, explore, and critically think about the history behind the American Experiment, the ideas that led to its rapid failure, how this failure has been carefully downplayed to prevent action, and how political participation is necessary in order to make change a reality.

COLONIALISM, NEO-COLONIALISM AND THE STAINS OF GENOCIDE

The term "colonialism" is possibly one of the most perplexing, if not contested concepts in the study of political science and of society at large. Most Americans would likely be hard-pressed to reference it beyond the "colonial period" of U.S. history when early European immigrants established their colonies in the New World. The postulation since the founding of the United States has been that everyone born within the national boundaries is considered an American citizen with equal rights, whether or not they consent to such citizenship. In this regard, the United States is normalized as the ascendant power to which all citizens, indigenous and non-indigenous, are subject. Although, in theory, a democracy "of the people, by the people, and for the people," the nation's unofficial yet authentic history of imperialism does not match its declared democratic principles. Namely, neo-colonialism that is defined as the efforts to use political, social, and economic controls for former dependent nations.

Colonialism, as we know it today, as a concept has its roots in European expansion and the so-called founding of the New World. The European powers of the British, French, Dutch, Portuguese, Spanish, and others established colonies in lands they "discovered" in order to facilitate trade and extract resources (natural resources and the kidnapping and sale of people). This can be characterized as the earliest stages of what we now call globalization. These "mother" countries dominated indigenous populations through their colonial regimes despite the higher numbers of indigenous people. The most conspicuous examples are in Africa, for example, the Dutch colonies in South Africa, the French in Algeria, Asia, and the Pacific Rim, and the British in India and Fiji.

Beginning in the 1940s, the world saw a wave of decolonization throughout many of Europe's colonies as indigenous populations fought wars of resistance against their foreign rulers. Mahatma Gandhi emerged as one of the world's greatest heroes for leading India's fight against the British. Likewise, Nelson Mandela is celebrated worldwide as a liberation fighter for South Africa where he was once considered a terrorist. In these instances, European regimes were pressured to pack up and return home, relinquishing political control to the indigenous population.

In many places, colonial incursion decimated indigenous populations through disease and military incursions to the point where if the indigenous population survived at all, it became the minority while the settler population became the majority. The largest examples of this are in North and South America, the Caribbean islands, New Zealand, Australia, and Israel.

Settler colonialism has been best explained as more of an imposed structure than a historical event. This structure is characterized by relationships of ascendance and subjugation that become woven throughout the fabric of society, ultimately becoming dissimulated as paternalistic benevolence. The objective of settler colonialism is always the acquisition of indigenous territories and resources, which require the native population to be displaced and eliminated. This can be accomplished in overt ways, including biological warfare and military action, but also in more subtle ways; for example, through national policies of assimilation.

As philosophical thinker, Patrick Wolfe has argued, the logic of settler colonialism is to eradicate the incumbent culture in order to supersede it. Assimilation involves the systematic divesting away of indigenous culture and replacing it with that of the new or "superior" culture. One of the ways this occurred in the United States was through racialization.

Racialization is the process of quantifying cultural and physical characteristics in terms of blood degree and hierarchy of races within a species; when indigenous people intermarry with non-indigenous people, they are verbally and socially expressed to lower their blood quantum or social relevance. This is because their indigenous (Indian or Native American) influence has marked them.

According to this logic, when enough intermarriage has occurred, there will be no more natives within a given lineage. It does not take into account personal identity predicated on cultural affiliation or other markers of cultural heritage.

Other ways in which the United States carried out its assimilation policies include the allotment of native lands, coerced enrollment in Indian boarding schools, termination and relocation programs, the bestowal of American citizenship, and Christianization.

BRIEF OVERVIEW OF INDIGENOUS HISTORY

© Everett Collection/Shutterstock.com

For some of us, we don't consider when indigenous history started in the America's. First off, so much of their history was destroyed between the Pequot War, the Trail of Tears, and the Native American Removal Acts there was not much history left outside of what was held by the elders.

Because this land was stolen, the indigenous (meaning original people from this land prior to the European invasion) had their own culture, forms of commerce (trade), and spirituality. As we now know, the experience of colonization in the new United States of America was bloody, racist, and based on religious beliefs of a new world and manifest destiny.

The indigenous peoples who originally inhabited the land that is now called "The United States" have had a complex history with the new settlers who would eventually establish their government here. Though many people still celebrate Columbus Day and Thanksgiving as though these holidays mark the beginning of a beautiful, mutually beneficial relationship between Native Americans and European settlers, these days are actually indicative of how much the history has been altered to fit a nationalistic template that paints the settlers as benevolent, if not a bit hapless, wanderers who accepted help whenever they could and paid it forward once they had a better idea of the "New World."

By the time state governments started emerging and gaining traction, many states passed laws that stripped Native Americans of their rights and extended their jurisdiction into many of the tribe's lands. Much like African-Americans in the United States or, more accurately, anyone who was not a white male, Indigenous people were treated horribly including, but not limited to, slavery, torture, and genocide. Once the colonies won their independence in 1776, the mistreatment became legal and sanctioned by the U.S. government, which included coordinated military responses for removal.

At the early phases of the Western European invasion, the America's (or the colonies) consisted of thirteen territories where slavery and genocide were regular acts of successful citizenship and economic wisdom. Groups of people from various parts of Europe arrived to inhabit land that in most cases were already inhabited by other people. The memory and history of the indigenous people of the Americas have been erased from the American narrative. These were civilizations of people that had culture, language, religion, and science thousands of years before the Europeans arrived. Hundreds of thousands of men, women, and children were killed without thought in the name of expansion.

Two examples of direct forms of genocidal behavior are the gifting of small pox-infested blankets from European colonizers to Native Americans in order to bring the fatal disease into their communities. European colonizers terrorized Native Americans for centuries as they made their way across the country to California (1807–1912). Another example is the infamous Indian Removal Act (1830). This was implemented during the democratic President Andrew Jackson's administration. In an effort to provide land to wealthy white Europeans in the North and the South, government leaders felt the need to remove the Native Americans from their land in an "agreeable" manner. Although not agreeable by the indigenous people, non-native people were in support of such measures.

The Indian Removal Act was preceded by an 1823 Supreme Court decision (1823) which stated that Indians could stay on land within the United States, but they could not hold a deed or title to that land. This made it possible for Europeans to take the land away from Native Americans without recourse. Indigenous communities did not have equal protection under the law. The five major tribes that were impacted by the removal acts were the Cherokee, Chickasaw, Choctaw, Muscogee (Creek), and Seminole Nations. The migration of thousands of Native Americans across the country led to what is known as the Trail of Tears.

Throughout the installation of the American government, indigenous peoples seemed like an inconvenience that the new Euro-Americans did not understand, though they did not need to understand, and considered utterly backward in their traditions. Among the many heinous actions the U.S. government took against the Native American tribes, the forceful removal from their homes was among the most devastating. In favor of white settlement, the Indian Removal Act of 1830 was signed by former President Andrew Jackson and required that the Civilized Nations, any nation east of the Mississippi River, relinquish their lands. Although the removal was implied by law to be voluntary, the nations were at a legal disadvantage in many of the negotiations regarding the retention of their land.

© Allison C Bailey/Shutterstock.com

This passage included the Trail of Tears, a particularly arduous journey the Cherokee nation took from their original lands in the southeastern region of the United States to a designated Indian territory, what is now Oklahoma. Between 1838 and 1839, the journey cost 4,000 lives and greatly influenced how Native Americans would be subsequently treated with regard to what lands they were allowed to live on. Although the Supreme Court cases, Cherokee Nation v. Georgia (1831) and Worcester v. Georgia (1832), Chief Justice John Marshall ruled that the Supreme Court and individual states do not have jurisdiction over native nations. The cases also mentioned that any land that was originally inhabited by the indigenous peoples as part of the United States, giving the federal government free-reign to enforce the removal policies through force and manipulation.

As indigenous peoples made their way to various Midwestern and Western States, there was a new American intrusion decision to be made by the U.S. government. How to best corral and regulate the natives into easy to manage areas to better enforce the idea that America has authority? The Indian Appropriation Act of 1851 under former President Millard Fillmore was established as a reservation system for the native tribes so that there were no disputes regarding territory and, in a perfect display of white privilege, "civilize" them to the American way. The Cherokee Nation is now currently located in Western North Carolina after another series of migrations through the years. Through a number of treaties between native nations and the United States, there are over three hundred reservations in the U.S., offering indigenous people some sovereignty.

https://drcryscrain.medium.com/buried-leads-missing-murdered-indigenous-women-mmiw-9d77818a0bd2

AMERICAN REVOLUTION IN CONTEXT OF SLAVERY

At the dawn of the American Revolution, 20 percent of the population in the thirteen colonies were of African descent. The legalized practice of enslaving blacks occurred in every colony, but the economies of the Southern colonies perpetuated the institution, which was first legalized in Massachusetts in 1641. During the Revolutionary era, more than half of all African Americans lived in Virginia and Maryland. Most blacks lived in the Chesapeake region, where they made up more than 50 to 60 percent of the overall population. The majority, but not all, of these African Americans were slaves. In fact, the first official United States Census taken in 1790 showed that only 8 percent of the black populace were free.

Attitudes and class structures legitimized a slave system predicated on the color of a person skin, or social status. Slavery permeated virtually all aspects of American life in 18th-century Virginia. Beginning with the advent of the first Africans at Point Comfort in 1619, an initially extemporaneous system of hereditary bondage for blacks gradually developed. Over the course of 150 years, slavery became entrenched in Virginian society, increasingly fortified by a series of restrictive laws and reinforced by the edifications of the community and family. Slavery was the substructure of Virginia's agricultural system, and it was essential to its economic viability. Initially, planters bought slaves primarily to raise tobacco for export.

By the last quarter of the 18th century, affluent Virginia farmers were utilizing slave labor in a diversified agricultural regime. Enslaved black people worked as tradesmen in the countryside and in the capital city of Williamsburg.

Burning of McIntosh at St. Louis, in April, 1836.

© Everett Collection/Shutterstock.com

Many others toiled as domestics in the households of wealthier white Virginians. The constant interaction between black slaves and white "masters" (as well as blacks and whites in general) engendered an interdependence that led to the development of a distinctive Virginian culture. This interdependence was as destructive as it was unequal.

The horrors endured by enslaved African Americans, whether physical or noetic, were numerous. White Virginians were caught up in a system that equated success with ownership of slaves. Economic reliance on slavery, fears about the consequences of emancipation, and unyielding racial prejudice all contributed to the continuation of slavery beyond American independence from the British. This fight for independence from the British did not extend to people of color and indigenous communities.

THE U.S. CONSTITUTION

Written in 1787, ratified in 1788, and in operation since 1789, the U.S. Constitution has served as a beacon of hope for the dream that is America. Its first three words—"We the People"—affirm the dream of a nation-state that accommodates its citizens. This accommodation can come through the form of political representation, taxation, services, and infrastructure, as well as equal protection under the law.

The injustice for many Americans today is the failure of history books to portray an accurate and rigorous narrative that includes all people's experience, not just that of the victor. This short-sighted narrative has given us the foundation for a nation full of apathy and misunderstanding that the founding of this nation was not based on fostering true equality.

The "people" that our Constitution was written to protect were white heterosexual property-owning males. This legacy lingers in our social, economic, and political systems today as we struggle for justice and equal protection under the law. The phrase, "all men are created equal" provides a view into exactly who was considered a citizen at the time.

One could also speculate that many of our current misgivings and false interpretations of power can be derived from this inadequate representation of equality.

Currently people can assert their power through their elected representatives and the enumerated rights outlined in the constitution. This right is granted in Article I, which allows for a body of elected officials to be formed as a Congress consisting of a Senate and a House of Representatives. The Legislative Branch, in relation to the Executive and Judicial Branches, sit as the "First Branch" of the federal government.

The right to peaceably assemble, Amendment 1 (Bill of Rights) is often left to the interpretation of the state (or better yet agents of the state) and not the general populous. This was made evident during Occupy Wall Street Movement when thousands of people took the streets peacefully. Their encampments were considered a public nuisance by the state and businesses. While some business, in Oakland in particular, reported an increase in business, others in places like New York reported increased vandalism. Neither report emphasized the real question. If there are violent protestors that is a different level of questioning and "allowances" then if we are talking about peaceful protesters which was about 99 percent of those who showed up, I not more. These convenient over simplifications don't allow us to see that our rights are being dwindled right before our eyes.

The Constitution assigned responsibility to Congress for organizing the Executive and Judicial Branches, raising revenue, declaring war, and making all laws indispensable for executing these potencies. The President is sanctioned to veto categorical legislative acts, but Congress has the ability to override presidential vetoes by a two-thirds majority of both houses. The Constitution dictates that the Senate advises and gives consent on key executive and judicial appointments and on the ratification of treaties.

INTERPRETATIONS OF THE CONSTITUTION

The Constitution gives the Senate the power to confirm Supreme Court judges. This is a major component of our checks and balances system which makes our government somewhat unique. The Senate confirmation process reflects the issues and concerns of the committee reviewing presidential nominations. The process to become a judge on the Supreme Court is important as it holds great value to the contemporary interpretation of the Constitution.

For example, in 2006, Michigan voters approved a ballot initiative that banned an interpretation of the use of Affirmative Action. The initiative barred publicly funded colleges from granting "preferential treatment to any individual or group on the basis of race, sex, color, ethnicity or national origin." The case that inspired this ruling involved a white female applicant to the University of Michigan Law School who sued the school for discrimination after being denied entry. Interestingly enough, the interpretation that white people can be discriminated against because they aren't people of color is a baffling perspective on the issue, especially considering the goal of Affirmative Action is to develop parity due to the acknowledged historical conditions that created an unequal society for people of color that persists to this day.

None of this was discussed when it was only women considered for equalizing measures through the legislative process. Kohn (2013) doesn't see the dividing line between providing open access to women in employment and education, and the comparable need to sustain access for people of color. Her perspective is also valid due to the historical context of Affirmative Action, which was to enhance women's access to the workplace. Kohn (2013) admits that Affirmative Action has benefited white women more than any demographic group. In April 2014, the Supreme Court held that the ban could remain because the voters allowed it to persist through over 50% of the vote in 2006. "The justices found 6–2 that a lower court did not have the authority to set aside the measure approved in a 2006 referendum supported by 58% of voters." The question was twofold—would a different decision by the Supreme Court change the validity of statewide ballot initiatives, and would a discriminatory measure, regardless of the voters' appeal, remain valid to the Supreme Court? This debate is still alive and well in our political spheres. For over two centuries, the Constitution has remained relevant because the ability to challenge the law is written into the system. This allows for our current culture and society to continue challenging our institutions and making "we the people" accountable to protect our most vulnerable citizens. It is our responsibility to continue this struggle.

BILL OF RIGHTS
AND ADDITIONAL AMENDMENTS

BILL OF RIGHTS - 1791

Amendment 1

Congress shall make no law respecting an establishment of religion, or prohibiting the free exercise thereof; or abridging the freedom of speech, or of the press; or the right of the people peaceably to assemble, and to petition the Government for a redress of grievances.

Amendment 2

A well regulated Militia, being necessary to the security of a free State, the right of the people to keep and bear Arms, shall not be infringed.

Amendment 4

The right of the people to be secure in their persons, houses, papers, and effects, against unreasonable searches and seizures, shall not be violated, and no Warrants shall issue, but upon probable cause, supported by Oath or affirmation, and particularly describing the place to be searched, and the persons or things to be seized.

Amendment 6

The First Amendment provides several rights protections: to express ideas through speech and the press, to assemble or gather with a group to protest or for other reasons, and to ask the government to fix problems. It also protects the right to religious beliefs and practices. It prevents the government from creating or favoring a religion.

Amendment 8

Excessive bail shall not be required, nor excessive fines imposed, nor cruel and unusual punishments inflicted.

Amendment 9

The enumeration in the Constitution, of certain rights, shall not be construed to deny or disparage others retained by the people.

Amendment 3

No Soldier shall, in time of peace be quartered in any house, without the consent of the Owner, nor in time of war, but in a manner to be prescribed by law.

Amendment 5

No person shall be held to answer for a capital, or otherwise infamous crime, unless on a presentment or indictment of a Grand Jury, except in cases arising in the land or naval forces, or in the Militia, when in actual service in time of War or public danger; nor shall any person be subject for the same offence to be twice put in jeopardy of life or limb; nor shall be compelled in any criminal case to be a witness against himself, nor be deprived of life, liberty, or property, without due process of law; nor shall private property be taken for public use, without just compensation

Amendment 7

In Suits at common law, where the value in controversy shall exceed twenty dollars, the right of trial by jury shall be preserved, and no fact tried by a jury, shall be otherwise re-examined in any Court of the United States, than according to the rules of the common law.

Amendment 10

The powers not delegated to the United States by the Constitution, nor prohibited by it to the States, are reserved to the States respectively, or to the people

ADDITIONAL AMENDMENTS 1795-1933

Amendment 11 - Suits Against States

Amendment 13 - Abolition of Slavery and Involuntary Servitude

Amendment 15 - Voting Rights

Amendment 16 - Federal Income Tax

Amendment 18 - Prohibition

Amendment 12 - Election of President and Vice-President

Amendment 14 - Protects rights against state infringements, defines citizenship, prohibits states from interfering with privileges and immunities, requires due process and equal protection, punishes states for denying vote, and disqualifies Confederate officials and debts

Amendment 17 - Popular Election of Senators

Amendment 19 - Women's Right to Vote

Amendment 20 - Commencement of Presidential Term and Succession

ADDITIONAL AMENDMENTS 1933-PRESENT

Amendment 21 - Repeal of 18th Amendment (Prohibition)

Amendment 23 - District of Columbia Presidential Vote

Amendment 25 - Presidential Vacancy, Disability and Inability

Amendment 22 - Two-Term Limitation on Presidency

Amendment 24 - Abolition of Poll Tax Requirement in Federal Elections

Amendment 26 - Right to Vote at Age 18

Amendment 27 - Congressional Compensation

Source: https://www.u-s-history.com/pages/h926.html & https://www.archives.gov/files/legislative/resources/education/bill-of-rights/images/handout-3.pdf

BLACK PANTHER PARTY 10 POINT PLAN

We Want Freedom
We Want Power to Determine the Destiny of Our Black Community.

We Want Full Employment for Our People
We believe that the federal government is responsible and obligated to give every man employment or a guaranteed income. We believe that if the White American businessmen will not give full employment, then the means of production should be taken from the businessmen and placed in the community so that the people of the community can organize and employ all of its people and give a high standard of living.

We Want An End to the Robbery By the Capitalists of Our Black Community.
We believe that this racist government has robbed us, and now we are demanding the overdue debt of forty acres and two mules. Forty acres and two mules were promised 100 years ago as restitution for slave labor and mass murder of Black people. We will accept the payment in currency which will be distributed to our many communities. The Germans are now aiding the Jews in Israel for the genocide of the Jewish people. The Germans murdered six million Jews. The American racist has taken part in the slaughter of over fifty million Black people; therefore, we feel that this is a modest demand that we make.

We Want Decent Housing Fit For The Shelter of Human Beings.
We believe that if the White Landlords will not give decent housing to our Black community, then the housing and the land should be made into cooperatives so that our community, with government aid, can build and make decent housing for its people.

We Want All Black Men To Be Exempt From Military Service.
We believe that Black people should not be forced to fight in the military service to defend a racist government that does not protect us. We will not fight and kill other people of color in the world who, like Black people, are being victimized by the White racist government of America. We will protect ourselves from the force and violence of the racist police and the racist military by whatever means necessary.

We Want Education for Our People That Exposes The True Nature Of This Decadent American Society.
We Want Education That Teaches Us Our True History And Our Role in the Present-Day Society. We believe in an educational system that will give to our people a knowledge of self. If a man does not have knowledge of himself and his position in society and the world then he has little chance to relate to anything else.

We Want An Immediate End to Police Brutality and the Murder of Black People.
We believe we can end police brutality in our Black community by organizing Black self-defense groups that are dedicated to defending our Black community from racist police oppression and brutality. The Second Amendment to the Constitution of the United States gives a right to bear arms. We therefore believe that all Black people should arm themselves for self-defense.

We Want Freedom For All Black Men Held in Federal, State, County and City Prisons and Jails
We believe that all Black People should be released from the many jails and prisons because they have not received a fair and impartial trial.

We Want Land, Bread, Housing, Education, Clothing, Justice And Peace.
When, in the course of human events, it becomes necessary for one people to dissolve the political bands which have connected them with another, and to assume, among the powers of the earth, the separate and equal station to which the laws of nature and nature's God entitle them, decent respect of the opinions of mankind requires that they should declare the causes which impel them to the separation. We hold these truths to be self-evident, that all men are created equal; that they are endowed by their Creator with certain inalienable rights; that among these are life, liberty, and the pursuit of happiness. That, to secure these rights, governments are instituted among men, deriving their just powers from the consent of the governed; that, whenever any form of government becomes destructive of these ends, it is the right of the people to alter or abolish it, and to institute a new government, laying its foundation on such principles, and organizing its powers in such form, as to them shall seem most likely to effect their safety and happiness. Prudence, indeed, will dictate that governments long established should not be changed for light and transient causes; and, accordingly, all experience hath shown that mankind is more disposed to suffer, while evils are sufferable than to right themselves by abolishing the forms to which they are accustomed. But, when a long train of abuses and usurpations, pursuing invariably the same object, evinces a design to reduce them under absolute despotism, it is their right, it is their duty, to throw off such government, and to provide new guards for their future security.

We Want All Black People When Brought to Trial To Be Tried In Court By A Jury Of Their Peer Group Or People From Their Black Communities
As Defined By the Constitution of the United States.
We believe that the courts should follow the United States Constitution so that Black people will receive fair trials. The Fourteenth Amendment of the U.S. Constitution gives a man a right to be tried by his peer group. A peer is a person from a similar economic, social, religious, geographical, environmental, historical, and racial background. To do this the court will be forced to select a jury from the Black community from which the Black defendant came. We have been, and we are being, tried by all-White juries that have no understanding of the "average reasoning man" of the Black community.

Source: Black Panther Party Plan: https://www.blackpast.org/african-american-history/primary-documents-african-american-history/black-panther-party-ten-point-program-1966/

REFERENCES

Jillson, C. (2013) American Government: Political Development and Institutional Change. Routledge. London, United Kingdom.

Kohn, S. (2013) Affirmative Action Has Helped White Women More Than Anyone Retrieved from: https://ideas.time.com/2013/06/17/affirmative-action-has-helped-white-women-more-than-anyone/

IMPORTANT FACTS AND TERMS

Annapolis Convention: In September 1786, a regional meeting took place in Annapolis, Indiana that was meant to revise the Articles of the Confederate. However, the delegates present decided that, because the Articles of the Confederate was not adequate for the national issues that they needed to address, they would decide to reconvene in Philadelphia, Pennsylvania eight months later, which is where the present Constitution was drafted.

Anti-Federalists: A group of people who opposed the ratification of the Constitution in favor of the weak central government that was laid out by the Articles of the Confederate. They are famous for "The Anti-Federalist Papers," which are a collection of essays written to argue why they believed that the Constitution should not be adopted.

Articles of Confederation: The first Constitution of the United States, which was originally adopted on November 15, 1777. It was not adopted by the first thirteen states until March 1, 1781. The Articles made a loose confederation of the sovereign states and a weak central government, making each state government more powerful.

Bill of Rights: The first ten amendments of the Constitution of the United States.

Boston Massacre: A massacre that took place on March 5, 1770 in Boston that resulted in a squad of British soldiers murdering five citizens, including a black soldier named Crispus Attucks. It was a major precipitant to the Revolutionary War.

Boston Tea Party: An act of political resistance against the British that took place on December 16, 1773, as a result of the Tea Tax that would be levied by Great Britain should any tea from Britain land in America. The Boston citizens decided to sabotage the shipments of tea so that they would not be taxed. Along with the leaders of the Patriot movement, many citizens helped to unload the ships of the 342 crates of tea and dump them into the Boston Harbor. The Boston Tea Party was another event that worked as a strong catalyst for the American Revolution.

Checks and balances: The system by which the government is separated into three branches that have the authority to prevent actions by another branch of the government. In the United States, the separate branches are the executive (President), legislative (Congress), and judicial (Supreme Court). However, there are various loopholes that allow branches to make actions that another branch may not approve.

Confederation Congress: The successor to the Second Continental Congress, the Confederation Congress existed from 1781 to 1789 and consisted of delegates appointed by state legislatures.

Constitutional Convention: The Constitutional Convention was the follow up meeting to the Annapolis Convention. Taking place in 1787 in Philadelphia, the Constitutional Convention is the meeting where the Founding Fathers debated about the amendments that should be in the Constitution.

Continental Congress: Congress, as we know it today, is actually the third iteration. The First Continental Congress was a meeting of nine of the colony's delegates at Carpenter's Hall in Philadelphia in 1774 to discuss how to best demonstrate their authority against British Forces. The Second Continental Congress reconvened in May 1775 to plan their attack as the British Redcoats stormed Boston.

Declaration of Independence: Drafted by Thomas Jefferson between June 11 and June 28 and adopted on July 4, 1776, the Declaration of Independence is a document that marks the beginnings of the United States of America as an independent country instead of a British colony.

Declaratory Act: An act written by the British Parliament in 1776 that declared that, in lieu of repealing the Sugar and Stamp Acts, which taxed the uses of these goods, Great Britain would have complete authority and dominion over the American colonies. This act included certain provisions, particularly that which suspended the New York Assembly, which alarmed colonists and greatly encouraged them to want complete autonomy from Britain.

Era of Good Feelings: The short period of time between 1817 and 1825 during President Monroe's administration after the War of 1812 effectively ended the Federalists' reign, and the Democratic-Republican Party had government dominance and, essentially, ended the two-party system. However, internal disagreements caused the Democratic-Republican Party to split into two new parties during the 1824 elections, the Democrats and the National Republican Party.

Federalism: A system of government where one single territory is governed by two levels of government. For example, California is ruled under California and federal law.

Federalists: The politicians who were in agreement with ratifying the Constitution. They are responsible for "The Federalist Papers," which explains their beliefs about why the Constitution is necessary for American autonomy.

Inherent powers: Powers that are explicitly laid out for the government in the Constitution or can be reasonably justified implicitly. This allows the government to, in many ways, decide that they have a good deal of power that may not need, depending on how they choose to interpret the Constitution.

Intolerable Acts: A collection of acts that were enforced by the British immediately after the Boston Tea Party. The Massachusetts Government Act essentially neutralized any localized government that had been created and made Massachusetts a crown colony under General Thomas Gage. The Boston Port Bill closed the Boston Harbor until Massachusetts paid for the damages of the ruined tea. The Administration of Justice Act was essentially legalized police brutally, protecting British soldiers against charges if they were to hurt American citizens during law enforcement procedures. The fourth Coercive Act allowed British troops to occupy American dwellings.

Manifest Destiny: Immediately after American independence and the War of 1812, nationalist pride was at an all-time high, which inspired pioneers to desire westward expansion toward the Pacific Ocean. A major tenet of this particular wish was the idea of racial integrity and superiority, which allowed for the cruel mistreatment of indigenous peoples. This mindset was called "Manifest Destiny."

New Jersey Plan: A proposal for state representation that was an answer to the Virginia Plan. The New Jersey Plan was meant to give smaller states a fair representation in government proceedings by allowing all states to have equal voting rights in a unicameral (one legislative body) government.

Representative government: A system of government where citizens elect delegates to represent them in national governmental proceedings.

Republican government: A government that consists of the people. This type of government is in direct opposition to a monarchy or an aristocratic government.

Shays's Rebellion: A name given to a series of acts in 1786 and 1787 by farmers from New Hampshire to South Carolina, which were particularly serious in Massachusetts. The rebellion was in direct opposition to a series of taxes and debt collections imposed by the state and local law enforcement that made it difficult for farmers to make a living, especially as a result of bad crops and a difficult economic depression. The rebellion took its name from its symbolic leader, Daniel Shays of Massachusetts, a former captain of the Continental army.

Stamp Act Congress: The First Congress that convened as a result of the Stamp and Sugar Acts that were enforced by the British Parliament. The meeting was meant to show a unified authority to British Parliament and to try to get the Acts repealed. However, the individual rebellions enacted by citizens was more successful in seeing that the Sugar and Stamp Acts were repealed, as is common with many modern rebellions compared to Congress.

Virginia Plan: A proposed method of government where each state would have representative delegates in the national Congress that would be determined by the state's population. This form of delegation was a major disadvantage for smaller states.

Chapter 1

ENVIRONMENT AND ENERGY

2020 was the second-worst year for wildfires on recent record, with over 10 million acres burned.

Wildfires burned an average of 7 million acres per year in the 2010s, more than twice the annual average in the 1990s. Final data on 2020 wildfires will be released in March 2021.

https://usafacts.org/state-of-the-union/energy-environment/

Cultural Norms: Developing Personal and Political Agency

The American Dream is a social and cultural phenomenon that has taken hold in many people's beliefs about the guarantees of upward mobility in the U.S. The so-called American Dream implies that if you work hard and play by the rules you'll be rewarded by society (Peterson-Iyer, 2021). This pursuit has fueled incredible "rags-to-riches" stories that provide a hope that one day everyone will be rich. The lack of integrity of this cultural value is rarely questioned, and when it is, it's considered socialist. Any talk of economic justice, addressing the gender and racial pay gaps, and even free health insurance is discussed in the mainstream as a scoff against our *American way of life*. Meaning, profit over people instead of people over profit.

Our personal views on what we think we deserve, as people who live in the United States, doesn't only apply to our beliefs about the necessity of our capitalist economic system. Notions about economic life are a component of American political culture because of our representative democracy and tax system. We're a pay to play type of country. We invest our tax dollars and our elected or appointed leaders manage and govern our society.

How we our society is managed is influenced directly by our values – the dominant values and our collective beliefs. Why does the American political system of governance work so differently than most others? Politically astute French philosopher Alexis de Tocqueville, an early observer of American political culture, gave some answers during the 1830s. Tocqueville primarily came to the United States to answer the question, "Why are the Americans doing so well with democracy while France is having so much trouble?" During this period, France was in turmoil, swinging back and forth between absolutism and radical democracy. Tocqueville figured that France could learn a thing or two from the Americans, and his observations remain a critical perspective of American political culture to this day.

Tocqueville identified several factors that influenced America's prosperity, including abundant, fertile land, and countless opportunities for people to acquire it to make a living; a lack of a traditional feudal aristocracy; and a fiercely independent spirit, unhardened by frontier living.

THE AMERICAN IDEOLOGICAL BASE

The American political culture that Tocqueville described in the 1830s has transmuted over the years. Yet, in many ways, it has remained remarkably equipollent, even after the continent was settled coast to coast. Several familiar elements have characterized the American view:

Abraham Lincoln—Our political fondness comes from a narrative that places Lincoln as the heart of freeing enslaved black people in the United States.

Liberty—The belief in freedom that does not infringe on another person's ability to be free.

Equality—Because we live in a capitalist system, the equality many Americans advocate for is based on opportunity, which we still have to compete for. Competition is a major aspect of the American economic system.

Capitalism—An economic system that is said to promote competition and inspire innovation. Capitalism supports the economic divide that allows for there to be more workers than owners as profit being the motivation to keep the economy running. The wage–labor relationship between the working classes and the elites widens daily.

Democracy—We have a representative democracy. We are represented by elected and appointed officials that handle most public affairs.

Individualism—The rights that an individual has that are recognized by the state and collectively.

The Rule of Law—The belief that citizens will have equal protection under the law.

Nationalism—Nationalism is expressed with pride of a particular nations independence, or domination of others in their own self-interest. Regardless of the wrongdoings of the United States, many people still have pride in the country and the rhetorical values that are explained above.

Political socialization occurs when an individual starts to consciously or unconsciously integrate the political stratosphere by forming opinions, choosing a political party, and/or deciding which political actions or causes to spend time and energy on. These levels of discretion have a tremendous impact on how our society works.

Familial, socio-political, economic, racial, and educational background all play a role in what opinions a person may form. In many cases, these opinions will be also be heavily influenced by one's peers. At certain points in history, peers have had more political sway concerning specific issues than one's parents, religious leaders, and educational figures. One example would be white allies in the Civil Rights movement.

Although many white elders of the time were staunchly against racial integration and equal rights, there were a few moderates and liberals who knew that African-Americans deserved the same rights as any other American citizen. Despite accusations of "white guilt" and a self-serving need to rebel against authority casting a cloud over their motivations, white involvement in the movement supports the idea that a more inclusive political ideology can transcend the propaganda and archaic racist belief systems instilled into children and influence more positive socialization of political awareness.

Public opinion can be a strong determinant for what a person learns to accept as political truths or unacceptable lies. A child could grow up with politically active parents who attend protests and help to organize neighborhood activities meant to supplement or replace inadequate governmental programs. This child may learn to value the power of grassroots and alternative opportunities instead of trusting or relying on their government for assistance.

In other instances, a child who learned from parents and teachers that the government will always work out the various issues may adopt a passive "wait it out, and it will get better" attitude toward the government. The political socialization process is affected by these influences. The threat of being disowned by friends and family for differing political beliefs can be a significant deterrent in forming new political ideas.

There are many painful stories throughout the media that illustrate how teens and young adults have had to cope with the rejection from family and friends after making this seemingly personal yet political decision.

AGENTS OF SOCIALIZATION

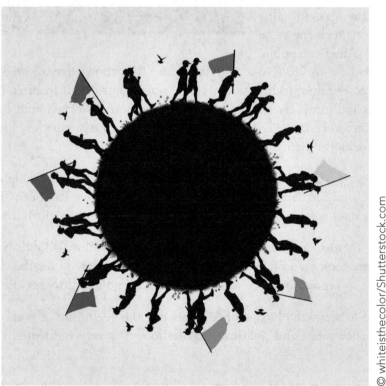

© whiteisthecolor/Shutterstock.com

Political socialization occurs over a person's lifetime. These influences vary between people and communities, providing information that is then used to create meaning and direction in our world. The concept of informed citizenship asks us to question the various factors that dictate the range of American political beliefs and the root intention of these influential people or events.

Bayard Rustin, an openly gay black man, and A. Phillip Randolph were the primary organizers of the infamous March on Washington for Jobs & Freedom. The march took place in August 1963. Attendees estimated that 250,000 to 350,000 people came to the event and that over 70% of the participants were black. Many people credit this march with helping to pass the Civil Rights Act of 1964 and subsequent bills in 1965. Why was it important for civil rights leaders to march to the Lincoln Memorial? How did the march's location impact public opinion and the ability of others to sympathize with civil rights issues?

© Jacob Lund/Shutterstock.com

The Lincoln Memorial resides in the District of Columbia as a symbol of national unification against slavery. This monument to Lincoln's legacy as a liberator has inspired hope for generations of Americans that the United States has the potential to be a truly equal nation. The choice to organize the march at the Lincoln Memorial was a tool utilized by the organizers because they knew that most Americans shared this romantic notion about Abraham Lincoln. This isn't to say that everyone feels the same about his legacy, but as American public figures go, he is the closest we have to a unifying hero. This knowledge allowed for the March on Washington for Jobs & Freedom to invoke emotional sentiments and it inspired critical questioning about the inequalities and injustices endured by black Americans, women, and other minorities. By connecting the contemporary struggle for civil rights with the Emancipation Proclamation, march organizers were able to anoint their cause with legitimacy.

Similarly, the rituals we participate in throughout our everyday lives play a significant role in our collective political socialization. Since 1892, the Pledge of Allegiance has been an effective method to instill loyalty to the national government and to foster a state of nationalism in the United States.

Originally crafted by Baptist minister Francis Bellamy for the National Public School Celebration, the Pledge of Allegiance took on a life of its own. See the figure below to see the various incarnations of this pledge. As early as kindergarten, American students are guided through an initiation of sorts.

Children are expected to recite the Pledge of Allegiance at the beginning of every school day. School serves as a place of major social and political socialization. It is very influential in shaping a child's identity.

Doing well at school is important for children; they are eager to please the adults in their lives, and adding the Pledge of Allegiance as an act found to please adults is a blurring of the lines between choice and coercion. In this regard, to be a good student also means one needs to be a good citizen. Following instructions and doing as they're told, including pledging allegiance to their country without any real understanding of what that means is a part of the nationalist induction.

Controversially, it could be argued that reciting the Pledge is also meant to squash any dissent among the people. The psychological process of memorizing and actually verbalizing the Pledge over a significant

EVOLUTION OF THE PLEDGE OF ALLEGIANCE

1892

(Crafted for the 1892 celebration of National Public School Celebration.

"I pledge allegiance to my Flag and the republic for which it stands, one nation indivisible, with liberty and justice for all."

1892-1922

"I pledge allegiance to my Flag and to the republic for which it stands: one nation indivisible, with liberty and justice for all."

1923

"I pledge allegiance to the Flag of the United States and to the republic for which it stands; one Nation indivisible with liberty and justice for all."

1924-1954

"I pledge allegiance to the Flag of the United States of America, and to the republic for which it stands; one Nation indivisible with liberty and justice for all."

1954- Present

(President Eisenhower encouraged Congress to add under God due to a perceived secular communist threat)

"I pledge allegiance to the Flag of the United States of America, and to the Republic for which it stands, one Nation *under* God, indivisible, with liberty and justice for all."

Source: Crystallee Crain

period of your life, sometimes 12 years, can leave a person confused when they find that they do not agree with the actions of their government. They may feel afraid to hold their government accountable, even for justifiable grievances.

I argue that the implementation of the Pledge of Allegiance in public schools presents a false choice for young people. It assumes that you, the citizen, have an active role or choice in deciding what your allegiance to the state should be. This idea is false in many ways. Human beings are sovereign beings; they thrived long before cities, states, and governments. We should not be forced to swear oaths to man-made institutions that do not meet our needs. But we do.

If the goal is to create and sustain national loyalty among its citizens, allowing for a voluntary pledge as a real choice would ensure authentic commitment rather than coercive and manipulative tactics to create a complacent citizenry.

Ask yourself:

Is it necessary to demand American children recite the Pledge of Allegiance every day? What are the benefits or disadvantages of it being used in public schools? Think about your experience in schools. Did you have to say it? Did your school give you the option to opt-out of participating for religious reasons? Talk with another student about why the Pledge of Allegiance is or isn't relevant to our democracy.

MANUFACTURING OF AMERICAN SOCIAL AND POLITICAL AGENCY

Politics is not only about the decisions governments make about access to resources, but understanding politics is also about psychological and social relationships to power, liberation, and change. Being in states of power or powerlessness is rooted in our relationship to one another and our relationship to the state. Oftentimes, these dynamics are out of our control, and we are often unknowingly propelled into a world of realities that we cannot explain or understand.

Many of us accept what is offered rather than ask questions. Why do we have such vast economic inequality? Why do we still engage in racist dialogues while we profess progress and the idea of a post-racial America? Why do we press for an ideological debate in favor of taxing the 1% while the rest of America blindly continues to allow them to suck the world dry at our collective expense? The contradictions are evident and sometimes paralyzing. But they don't have to be. Information is power, and you have the ability to change your communities and create the level of equality and fairness that will sustain generations to come.

Socialist Left

SL thinkers are against the status quo that creates and maintains inequity. SL thinkers work to dismantle injustice through a variety of means. Through elected office, grassroots organizing, and systems change. SL thinkers are heavily impactful as they are "systems" thinkers and believe that change can occur in any space. Socialist are being elected to office across the U.S. (2018) and have led social justice movements to organize the most marginalized.

Political Apathic

PA thinkers generally gravitate towards the opinion that participating in any election is "wasting" their vote. There is a social and political compulsion to remain neutral and resistant to committing to any particular stance on an issue. PA thinkers often perpetuate harm unknowingly by their lack of action and passive bystander position on harm that exists in the world.

Revolutionary Minded

RM thinkers are don't believe in the reformation of the system as we know it. Revolutionary thinkers believe that ending the system as we know it and starting over will be the best way to sustain our society. RM thinkers don't prescribe to incremental changes in social and political matters.

Radical Left

RL thinkers want to see big sweeping changes regarding social and political problems. Outraged by vast inequality, some RL thinkers believe aggressive strategies to show dissent are a valid response to state violence while others take a more passive or nonviolent approach. Both have equal value depending on the threat to humanity.

Conservative Moderate

CM thinkers believe in either no government or very limited government intervention into most social problems. They are advocates of low taxes and reduced state-offered social programming. To CM thinkers, more social programs equal more administration spending which means a bigger government. However, this same rationale does not apply to military or other defense spending.

Conservative Right

CR thinkers tend to resist change that diminishes historical truths they hold about the maintenance of their cultural or political power.
CR thinkers hold "traditional" values often associated with Christian religious norms. Many CR thinkers do not go along with contemporary conventional wisdom or even science when it comes to matters of a woman rights to choose, the idea of creationism, or health care.

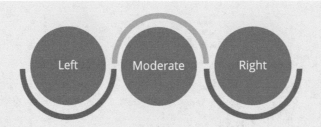

Liberal Left

LL thinkers generally disagree with any injustice in our social, economic, and political systems. They may display this disdain for the current system through corporate boycotts or online petitions, but their attachment to social and economic comfort enslaves them to incremental changes rather than large leaps of progress and collective liberation.

Liberal Moderate

LM thinkers are what social liberally and fiscally conservative people may call themselves. Socially liberal people may not want the government to dictate their private lives while fiscally conservative people resist the concept of tax liability for social programs. The difference between CM and LM thinkers is the focus on equality. Issues of disadvantage and privilege are not the primary framework for conservatives, while liberal conservatives people social programs are important..

Right Wind Reactionary

RWR thinkers view societal change and progress as a detriment to their livelihood and treat dissent or lack of unity on their viewpoints as a personal attack. RWR thinkers tend to use extreme and harmful methods against everyday people. They are known to create inflated scenarios of persecution and threats in order to justify their prejudices and maintain their own perceived status.

Source: Crystallee Crain

IMPORTANT FACTS AND TERMS

Agents of socialization: The individuals, groups, and institutions that help to build the context for a particular subject or group, which guides an individual into that group or subject. Examples of agents of socialization include family, friends, school, and the media. Each of these entities help to form a context for someone when they are first emerging into the political world.

Conservative: Often mistaken as simply Republican, conservative is that holds traditional values regarding fiscal and social issues. They believe in being cautious about social change and are steadfast about not using fiscal resources, even if it means cutting important national programs, such as welfare, social security, and Medicare.

Liberal: A political ideology, often in opposition to conservative values, especially as the media has covered the political dichotomy that values social evolution and using fiscal resources for social programs. While this is a noble effort, liberal programs often leave citizens overly dependent on the government instead of promoting social activism and self-sufficiency.

Moderate: A political opinion that lies in between conservative and liberal. A moderate may believe in progressive social issues but want the government to be fiscally responsible. On the other hand, a moderate may have traditional social beliefs but support governmental spending.

Neoconservatives: A group of people who believe that markets are an efficient and necessary means of distributing goods and services but are not complete supporters of free-market capitalism. Neoconservatives support inheritance tax, graduated income tax, and welfare.

Party identification: The political affiliation choice one makes to reflect their political beliefs.

Political culture: Widely shared beliefs, values, and traditions regarding a country's politics that have been part of that particular country's history and has shaped the context for much of political debates and discussions.

Political ideology: A strong belief or opinion regarding political values and actions, often particular to a specific group of people.

Political party: An affiliation term that determines one's political beliefs and their inclinations to vote for certain politicians and initiatives.

Political socialization: When an individual starts to integrate himself or herself into the political stratosphere by forming opinions, deciding which party to align him- or herself with, and what types of political actions would be more likely to result in their political goals being met.

Populist: Someone who supports the rights of the people.

Chapter 2

Prior to the pandemic, the poverty rate decreased from 15% in 2010 to 10.5% in 2019, the lowest it had been since 1980.

REFERENCES

Peterson-Iyer, K. (2021) Review: What happens when the American Dream doesn't measure up? Retrieved from: https://www.americamagazine.org/arts-culture/2021/08/06/hinze-economics-radical-sufficiency-241157

CHAPTER THREE

The Internet, Privacy, and Political Change

At the heart of any true democracy is the ability for citizens to express dissent peacefully and without censorship. To fully express grievances at the government level is a crucial element of our ability to be human in the eyes of the law. Our right to participate in the development of our nation is also enumerated as such in our Constitution. We have the right to address those public institutions that we feel need to be changed to serve the public best. Public officials and their staff are paid with tax dollars. This is our money and our contribution to the creation and maintenance of the system. If our taxes are used, it is fair to reason that our voices, ideas, and priorities should be equally valued.

Dissent in the United States varies, as does the experience of people who identify themselves as Americans. The types of problems that citizens choose to address publicly vary. Often, these forms of dissent are organized around an election or an issue area where citizens need to make a choice. When citizens join together to voice dissent, especially in regard to human rights and justice issues, the fervor can be palpable as people are infused with hope, inspiration, and a sense of excitement that political change is possible.

What does it mean to disobey? It means to act, think, and promote ideas that challenge the status quo. The motivation behind dissent comes from a deep desire for justice and equality. Conscientious objection is the refusal to participate in the perceived wrong taking place. This could include disobeying a law that is felt to be unjust. While breaking the law is not the ideal goal of the objector, it is a powerful method that demonstrates the drastic measure a person is willing to take to seek justice.

Civil disobedience in the United States varies as much as civic life is regulated. For example, to have a lawful protest, you must petition to have your rally or march approved by city officials or the police department in most municipalities. This level of "management" of traditional forms of civil disobedience in the United States sometimes compromises the people's ability to hold the government accountable. What if the police department or city happens to be the targeted audience of your message? Is it necessary to have the municipality regulate these activities, or should citizens have the right to "peaceably assemble" wherever necessary depending on the political situation?

In this section, we will explore the strategies used to create and maintain the power for the few (elites, powerful) at the cost of the many (voters, everyday people). More recently, we witnessed the political polarization during the 45th Presidency, with the left and right perspectives divided towns, states, and the entire nation.

The January 6, 2021, <u>insurrection</u> that took place at the U.S. Capitol was a blow to our democratic principles and the values of one vote, one person, one nation. In dissent toward the results of the 2020 election that named Joe Biden as our 46th President of the United States, supporters of the 45th President believed it was their "right" to storm the Capitol, cause death, and traumatize our nation by staging an insurrection. While there are currently over 200 people with criminal and civil indictments, there were also reports of staffers or members of <u>Congress</u> who participated. The FBI has the cooperation of dozens of local police departments to identify the participants in this violent act.

The actions of the insurrectionists ask us to consider a few questions:

1. *What are the limits to dissent in the United States?*
2. *Are the descriptors in the constitution "peaceably assemble" enough guidance to inform our democracy in different times and cultural contexts?*
3. *Who gets to decide if one form of dissent is more acceptable than another?*
4. *How do we monitor social media sites for extremism and hate speech while recognizing personal privacy and public safety?*
5. *How can we bridge the divides among people to cultivate our multi-cultural democracy?*
6. *What role does white supremacy play in our social and political lives?*

The aftermath of the insurrection has left many in Congressional leadership traumatized and afraid to go to work. The nation's moral compass was damaged, and in some ways, the full impact of what it means has been swept under the rug. A bipartisan Congressional committee has begun an investigation into the insurrection.

The response to the insurrections inspires others questions for us to consider:

1. *What is the role of Congress to hold themselves accountable for participating in insurrectionist violence against the United States?*
2. *How can we, as a country, heal from the January 6th insurrection?*
3. *How do we prevent false narratives about the true impact of the insurrection and how its represented in history books?*
4. *How can we hold people accountable for domestic terrorism? How do we prevent extremist violence?*
5. *How do we rebuild our country's morale and mend the divisiveness in our political and social culture?*

THE INTERNET AND SOCIAL CHANGE

The Internet has revolutionized communication and the process of sharing information. It is not only easier to dispense ideas and new facts, but it is also quicker and more likely to spark a discussion because of how many people a particular piece of information can reach in an instant.

© Vizilla/Shutterstock.com

For this reason, the Internet has become a new favorite tool in the game of politics. Politicians can use websites as a tool to spread their political platform and other messages. And more recently, social media sites are being used to broaden their base and deepen their influence.

Voters regularly go online to research, investigate, and discuss their beliefs and ideas with other like-minded as well as oppositional citizens, gaining a better idea of how to view various hot topics in the political climate. Grassroots organizers and protesters have taken to social media websites to flesh out the details of their next demonstration or organization meeting.

President Obama used Marshall Ganz's model of grassroots organization to help him win the 2008 campaign and engaged young voters through a strategic online process. As a result, he became the first president to harness the Internet's potential, fully outreaching to the public in a massive online campaign that almost certainly helped him win the presidency. On all fronts, the Internet has the potential to create a positive change within the political and social structure of the United States.

Yet, the political agenda still revolves around politicians arguing over issues that never seem to get any closer to achieving social justice, fair treatment, or civic responsibility. Mass media, which has come to include the Internet, television, radio, cinema, recordings, mobile phones, and print, has simply become a tool in the proliferation of falsehoods under the guise of "educating the public." What has resulted from this doctoring of information has been a dissemination of false truths, rumors, and propaganda that mislead the public by unfairly manipulating the public opinion of political affairs.

Because many websites do not require cited sources, it is also entirely possible to pass an opinion off as fact, which is dangerous when considering the topics that receive this treatment include abortion, immigration, education, globalization, LGBTQIA rights, environmental conservation, and wealth distribution, to name a few.

As the Internet and other forms of media have evolved, the ability to make fair decisions based on truth often becomes the casualty of a war on the acquisition and distribution of knowledge.

As advocates for political transparency and freedom of the press continue to defend the public's right to know, still corporations and agents of the government made various attempts that certain information is kept from the public. Amid conspiracies regarding weapons of mass destruction, the "9/11 Commission Report" was quietly released on July 22, 2004, to lackluster media coverage.

As more people utilize the Internet to educate themselves about the political climate, various agencies have suddenly become keen on "protecting United States citizens from cyber terrorism" by giving the National Security Agency (NSA) and the Federal Communications Commission (FCC) the authority to censor and silence many in the Internet community.

Although censorship of mass media has been an issue for many years, net neutrality is an example of how not only will the information on the Internet be distilled through lobbyists, interest groups, and corporate PACS, but it will become difficult to access the information at all. Ending net neutrality means that certain telecommunication companies, those which keep Washington in their pockets, will have monopoly control over the speed that people are allowed to use the Internet, effectively making it more or less challenging to educate themselves politically.

Mass media has always been controlled in some way. Ideally, it was meant to have unfettered distribution, a pure form of expressive freedom sent from the producer directly to the public. In reality, most avenues of mass media have been under a government and corporations control for years, and the Internet is no exception.

This chapter analyzes the role that the Internet has played in our lives to date and explores how it has been used to manipulate public perception of political developments. Challenging these assumptions will hopefully result in further introspection on how we can work together to ensure that the Internet remains a tool for freedom of the press and obtaining knowledge.

FREEDOM OF PRESS: THE TRUE MEANING OF DEMOCRACY

© TypoArt BS/Shutterstock.com

10 TACTICS
CLOSING AN OPEN
SOCIETY - NAOMI WOLFF

Invoke a terrifying internal and external enemy

Create a gulag

Develop a thug caste

Set up an internal surveillance system

Harass citizens' groups

Engage in arbitrary detention and release

Target key individuals

Control the press

Dissent equals treason

Suspend the rule of law

Source: https://www.huffpost.com/entry/ten-steps-to-close-down-a_b_46695

In her critical analysis of American politics, *The End of America*, by Naomi Wolff (2007) describes various tactics that the United States government has enacted to close our open society. In this best-selling book, she reveals a blueprint showing how once open societies can legally, and often, under the radar of ordinary citizens, actively participate in creating a closed culture that entraps them and removes civil liberties from all.

The End of America was inspired by Wolff's desire to return the political power back to the hands of the people. Where was the people's narrative in defining our resistance to maintain some level of ethical standards in our governance? The First Amendment of the Constitution regards freedom of the press. Amendment I states: "Congress shall make no law respecting an establishment of religion, or prohibiting the free exercise thereof; or abridging the freedom of speech, or of the press, or the right of the people peaceably to assemble, and to petition the Government for a redress of grievances."

A modern state enjoys healthy debate on politics and social issues openly to craft the best solutions possible for the greatest number of people. Arguably, the United States has enacted far too many restrictions to our First Amendment rights. Wolff indicates this as one of the steps taken to close an open society. How was this possible? After September 11, 2001, Congress felt a need to respond to the threat of terrorism quickly. Without many actual pieces of fact, the U.S. Congress passed on the most sweeping violations to civil liberties in the United States.

Some of the rationales for their actions were based on the need for "national security." The Uniting and Strengthening America by Providing Appropriate Tools Required to Intercept and Obstruct Terrorism, or USA Patriot Act of 2001, was one of the many measures enacted by Congress that removed civil liberties and violated many aspects of the Constitution. One in particular, our right to privacy and restrictions on the government for unreasonable search and seizure.

Some of the law's sanctioned actions include wiretapping, electronic surveillance, access to medical records, bank records, credit card statements, and individual library book records, all without requiring a warrant or even probable cause. The Patriot Act expanded federal law enforcement powers that have been used to dismantle many aspects of civil disobedience and freedom of speech and the press.

Politics in the United States is not a game of perfection. At its best, it's a methodology that should include an informed citizenry, a responsive electorate, and governmental leaders who respond to the needs of the people and are not influenced by corporate or special interests. Because special interests, often led by corporations—the rights of the individual and our access to information have been consistently thwarted.

IDEA—Read in a circle of friends and family silently or have one person read it aloud. When you're done, take some time to digest what he says and discuss your reactions.

Guerilla Open Access Manifesto
Aaron Swartz, July 2008, Eremo, Italy

IDEA—Read in a circle of friends and family silently or have one person read it aloud. When you're done, take some time to digest what he says and discuss your reactions.

Edward Snowden,
A Manifesto for the Truth
November 3, 2013 @ 6:24 pm
This article by Edward Snowden was published in Der Spiegel.

The democracy we experience day-to-day has been gifted to us, but it comes with a price. The price has been the people's lives and our time. Essentially thousands of days where American citizens and residents are working together and often against one another. However, I'd like to think that an engaged citizenry would afford equality as a central theme for their political process participation. Sadly, this is not true. Not all people believe that equity, justice, and freedom mean the same thing. This is the tricky part. The concept of people power has two dimensions—the first being the rights of the people that are expressed in the Constitution and the organizing efforts among the citizens to maintain and expand the interpretation of fairness, power, and dissemination of resources. The second dimension of people's power is the innate will to survive and live just lives. This is exhibited in our development and practice of personal and political agency. Personal agency is your individual will to lead your own life by a particular set of values. Political agency is your ability and interest in putting those values to work for a common goal or goodwill.

We are motivated by our's or other's personal experiences in relationship to the government and other systems. This helps us shape our perspective on what strategy we will use to create change in our political system.

Macedio et al. (2005) wrote:

> "American democracy is at risk. The risk comes not from some external threat but from disturbing internal trends: an erosion of the activities and capacities of citizenship. Americans have turned away from politics and the public sphere in large numbers, leaving our civic life impoverished. Citizens participate in public affairs less frequently, with less knowledge and enthusiasm, in fewer venues, and less equally than is healthy for a vibrant democratic polity" (p. 1).

REAGANOMICS—REAGAN'S RISE TO POWER

Famous for backing the trickle-down theory, championing elite conservative issues, and coining the term "welfare queen," Ronald Reagan has been the example of what good Republican values are since he was elected President in 1981. He'd been gaining momentum in politics for the previous decade, running against President Gerald Ford for the presidency in 1976, and then giving support to him once Ford gained the upper hand during the campaign. However, once he became president in 1981, there was no denying the political power that he had accrued since deciding to take a turn into politics from being a famous Hollywood actor, effectively showcasing how it is possible to win an election based solely on star power, good communication skills, and promising to make it easier for rich people to keep their money.

Throughout history, these have been unspoken tenets to any election. Though many people would point out these qualities in previous elections and campaigns as criticism or satirical comedy, there was still a measure of legitimacy to the previous candidates, at least because they had years of previous experience from a career in politics. President Reagan marked one of the first celebrities-turned-political figures in a new trend of popular people lending their expertise to politics, essentially taking advantage of people's affection for him as an actor rather than his political resume, experience, or ideologies as they relate to citizens.

It was during his presidency in the 1980's that the concept of trickle-down theory became a well-publicized economic strategy. Dubbed "Reaganomics," the trickle-down theory allows the elite to receive tax cuts with the assumption that it would serve as economic stimulus and "trickle-down" to those in the working class through job creation and more economic growth.

The ultimate result of Reaganomics was not that the rich created new jobs. The tax cuts meant that they were able to hold onto their money and wield more power in the political realm. Since then, though there have been modest tax increases across the board for all citizens, there is still a major disparity between the taxes lower and middle-class citizens have to pay and what the upper-middle and upper-class pay.

Furthermore, Reagan's economic legacy has contributed to the widening income disparity between the working class and the wealthy that has been steadily growing since Reaganomics went into effect. The trickle-down theory has been in wide use since then in many ways, including the reluctance that Congress has shown in raising the elite's taxes.

President Reagan also went down in infamy for labeling black women and other women of color, "welfare queens." Many people saw this as classist and racist as poverty was problematized and personalized. Reagan was key in drilling down the idea of the bootstrap mentality within a person's individual life.

We live in a country that has created policies that go against those who are increasingly being pushed out of urban centers due to gentrification—leaving many families without access to transportation, work, and viable education or vocational options for self-improvement. In the United States, we readily cut taxes for the wealthy while inflating the cost of goods (for the average person) and while also being more than reluctant to raise the minimum wage.

This, in addition to Nancy Reagan's campaign, titled the "War on Drugs," is responsible for the rising prison population in the last 30 years. The economic deregulation and the expansion of private-sector corporations influencing the government make a compelling case that the Reagan administration was primarily built around protecting elite white men and their interests.

IMPORTANT FACTS AND TERMS

Agenda-setting effect: The agenda-setting effect, coined by Walter Lippmann, is when the media covers political campaigns, decisions, and mistakes in a specific manner that changes the public's perception, response, and reality of what politicians are doing with their power. Because many media companies are affiliated with politicians, their coverage is often inaccurate and skewed to draw attention away from unethical political schemes and deeds.

Communications Act of 1934: The Communications Act of 1934 was signed into law during President Franklin D. Roosevelt's first presidency, which consolidated television, radio, and phone monitoring, forming the Federal Communications Commission (FCC). This act made it easier for the government to regulate what consumers were able to watch and communicate to one another through these various forms of media.

Doublespeak: A term often credited to, but not coined by, George Orwell's 1947 novel *Nineteen Eighty-Four* and refers to the technique of phrasing terms in a manner that is meant to confuse and distort events or situations. For example, a bank doesn't have "bad loans"—it has "non-performing assets."

Federal Communications Commission (FCC): The Federal Communications Commission (FCC) was established in 1934 and has been used as a regulation tool by the government, making it possible for them to push a federal agenda regarding what is appropriate for consumption and communication between responsible adults.

Framing effect: In 1981, Daniel Kahneman and Amos Tversky's research found that a person's perception of a specific topic could be altered simply by whether or not the information was presented with positive or negative contextual choices. This framing effect makes it possible for the media to change how a particular event or person would be perceived. An example would be how newspapers covered the survival efforts of those displaced by Hurricane Katrina. African-Americans were depicted as looters, while white people were described as scavenging for supplies.

Inverted Pyramid Model: The Inverted Pyramid Model is age-old media coverage technique that dictates that the most important information of any event or coverage in written media needs to be at the beginning of a piece while less cogent information must be at the end.

Muckraking tradition: A pre-World War I journalistic tradition of accurately reporting on the social and political corruption that permeated the American government and corporations. This form of investigative journalism helped to bring many scandals to light and influenced many governmental changes.

Objectivity: Objectivity is the ability to see an issue from a rational, impersonal perspective, retelling the events as they happened without the writer's perception or experience in the writing. In journalism and media, while this is useful in many ways, it also allows double meanings and doublespeak to become the default for how information is reported.

Partisan press: A method of assigning competing media outlets opposing political parties on which to report, effectively changing the way that many Americans perceive political actions, figures, or decisions.

Penny press: A form of newspaper that was able to reach more lower-class citizens in the 19th century because, instead of running for six cents as was the norm, it was only a penny. More Americans were, therefore, able to read the news and know what was happening in their government and society.

Persuasion effect: An effect where a reader or viewer will initially be more persuaded by a high credibility source, but after a few weeks, they will be equally persuaded by a low-credibility source. The persuasion effect is also referred to as "the sleeper effect." This effect implies that, eventually, it is possible to make anything sound legitimate when the right amount of time has passed after exposure to the information.

Buckley v. Valeo: A 1976 Supreme Court case that amended the Federal Election Campaign Act of 1971, as amended in 1974 and established the Federal Election Commission (FEC), that were deemed unconstitutional. The Supreme Court upheld that the FEC was constitutionally within its rights to limit the contributions any one candidate could receive in an election, disclose the provisions and records of the FECA, and public financing of Presidential elections. The case decided that limiting how much a candidate could spend, except the President who receives public funding, and how the FEC appoints members was unconstitutional.

Civil code: The statutes and laws that govern business and negligence lawsuits and practices.

Corporate personhood: The concept that a corporation can be recognized as an individual in the eyes of the law. This grants the corporation the same rights as an individual, often allowing the executives of the corporation to take advantage of various loopholes and further taking advantage of its employees and those who are affected by the corporation's decisions.

Full faith and credit clause: A phrase in Article IV, Section 1 of the Constitution which dictates that a larger American government entity can help to alleviate the debts of a smaller, less stable government entity of the United States. This particular act is reminiscent of the bank bailout that recently took place, considering many banks are unofficially considered governmental entities.

International Monetary Fund (IMF): Founded in 1944 and inspired by the Great Depression's effect on international economies, the International Monetary Fund (IMF) is in charge of monitoring and regulating international monetary transactions, which includes determining the exchange rate.

Labor exploitation: Taking advantage of people by forcing labor out of them for personal and economic gain.

North American Free Trade Agreement (NAFTA): The North American Free Trade Agreement (NAFTA) was signed into law in 1993 by former President Clinton went into effect on January 1, 1994 and essentially eradicated any tariffs on goods traded between the United States, Canada, and Mexico. NAFTA critics worried that American jobs would inevitably start funneling to Mexico, exposing Americans to unemployment and exploiting Mexican workers.

Open Door Policy: Notes written by former Secretary of State John Hay in 1899 to China, which encouraged China to allow different nations to trade with them without any regulations or tariffs, essentially keeping the door open for economic trade opportunities. Although China was unsure of this agreement because there was no apparent economic benefit, they accepted so as not to insult the United States.

Organization of Petroleum Exporting Countries (OPEC): An organization founded in 1960 to support the world leaders in oil-exporting. Essentially a who's who of all of the wealthiest nations. OPEC as a whole has a large influence on the overall economic outlook.

Santa Clara County v. Southern Pacific Railroad: An 1886 Supreme Court case wherein the Southern Pacific Railroad refused to pay taxes to Santa Clara County on the grounds that the Southern Pacific started in Missouri, so California has no rights to tax it. This case helped set a precedent for corporate personhood.

World Bank: Started in 1947 as part of the Marshall Plan to help rebuild Europe after World War II, the World Bank has been funding various government projects since then.

REFERENCES

Macedo, S. et al. (2005) *Democracy at Risk: How Political Choices Undermine Citizen Participation, and What We Can Do about It*. Washington D.C.: The Brookings Institute.
Wolff, N. (2007) Ten Steps to Close Down an Open Society. Retrieved from: https://www.huffpost.com/entry/ten-steps-to-close-down-a_b_46695

CHAPTER FOUR

The Erasure of the Vote, Interest Groups, and Political Campaigns

© 3dfoto/Shutterstock.com

Today, Republicans and Democrats make up our unofficial two-party system in the United States. Our Democracy has been put at risk, most recently in the 2016 and 2020 elections, where we saw massive interference of our elections by the Russian government. Their efforts included spreading false information to slander Hilary Clinton and dividing certain demographics, namely black voters and older voters. As well-known voting blocks in the United States, demographic-based propaganda and other covert acts were taken by a foreign government to dismantle our trust in our system. Some believe this is what got Donald Trump elected to the Presidency.

In the 2016 and 2020 elections, Bernie Sanders, who is an elected Independent from Vermont, ran as a Democrat in the national Presidential race. This shows that even those vying for power as an elected official are victim to this over simplification. During the campaign primaries in some states, if you are not a registered democrat or republican, you cannot vote in the primary. This is an egregious violation of democratic principles. In the wake of the 2020 election, Republican legislatures across the country protested the success of Biden's Presidential win by passing restrictive voting rights bills.

Currently, there are 28 bills in 18 states that move to restrict access to mail and absentee voting. Like one bill moving forward in Arizona, other efforts are being made to prevent elected officials from conducting voter registration drives on nongovernmental property. In New Hampshire, there are ten restrictive bills being pushed in the Legislature. Two of which target student voters by invalidating the use of university IDs as a valid photo ID for voting and requiring additional proof of residency affidavits.

The democratic and republican parties have been monopolizing the airwaves for years, debating over many important issues, hopefully with the public's best interests at heart. Any other political parties, such as the Green Party, the American Independent Party, the Libertarian Party, the Socialist Party, the Communist Party, the Peace and Freedom Party in California, and unaffiliated politicians and citizens that may appear on the ballot are considered to be a distraction or deviation from the norm. Democracy requires difference, yet our interpretation of it pushes for two "opposite" sides of a coin.

This two-party system ultimately alienates those who do not strictly adhere to their leanings, making it difficult to vote for changes that are necessary for citizens who identify with other parties. President Obama mentioning that, instead of voting as a Democrat or a Republican, it was more important to vote as an American who cares about change. This was idealistic at best. Before he took office as a Democratic president, Republicans were the first people at the podium to attack his residency and his birthright to be President, while Democrats staunchly defended him. The Republicans as the red states and the Democrats as blue states will remain a powerful media tool to help delineate between winning presidential and congressional elections. The media uses this as a way to show you where you are in comparison to the rest of the country.

HISTORY OF AMERICAN POLITICAL PARTIES

As American politics and culture has evolved, so have the core of the two political parties. Throughout history, the backing of a candidate is based on what the person represents their values are and how you believe they will enact those beliefs into policies and governance practice. When legally sanctioned slavery existed in public spaces, owners would vote for a politician who was anti-abolitionist because their endgame was earning as much money as possible. It was not unfashionable or illegal to not care about the humanity of the people they enslaved.

The same type of maintenance of affinity group occurs with as little care to their labor force's welfare as they could get away with by law. If one of their slaves died or they whipped a "lazy" slave until he or she died from shock, and they did not have to so much as pay a fine, then that was the best economic situation for them.

During and prior to the Civil Rights Movement, the status quo for many politicians who hoped to win a predominantly racist white male vote dictated that they adhere to pro-segregationist policies. In Alabama, Governor George Wallace was a local favorite because he promised to uphold a tradition of segregation and Jim Crow laws, even after desegregation became the political norm. More recently, the politician who wanted to win was the politician who endorsed the sentiment that corporations should be considered individuals for the benefit of the 1% or the obscenely rich. Interest groups are in place to make sure that these politicians get elected and are passing policies that specifically support their interests and causes. Oftentimes, this assurance comes with monetary motivation for politicians.

The power that interest groups have been able to wield in politics has grown to disproportionate levels. Throughout history, many interest groups were started as a means of representing those whose needs and desires were often unheard because of invisibility from racial, gender, economic, sociopolitical, and geographic disadvantages. Abolitionism would be one such example of an interest group that started as a means of representing slaves who legally could not represent themselves. Many labor rights movements and unions are interest groups that were meant to stop laws that allowed corporations to open company towns with worthless scrip, enforce unbearable hours, and maintain heinously unsafe working conditions that often claimed the lives of their workers. Although many of these groups have been fraught with corruption and internal disagreement in ideology, they attempted to remain true to their constituents—namely, those who were underrepresented and disadvantaged.

As corruption became more rampant within these interest groups and corporations started to gain more traction in this new social and political context, they found new loopholes that allowed them to increase their economic output through different, distinctly more nefarious, means. One of the most common methods that many interest groups utilize is lobbying, which is when a lawyer or representative essentially pleads the interest group's case to a politician regarding certain policies.

The National Rifle Association (NRA) is an example of an interest group that continues to have a heavy influence on many of the laws that are passed in the American government. While many gun control advocates, President Obama included, work toward passing laws that limit how firearms are distributed, who can purchase firearms, and the requirements for a gun license, there are still many standstills. Although the evidence suggesting that gun control is a major issue in our country—the United States has the most lenient gun control laws of all developed nations and 15 out of 25 of the worst mass shootings of the last 50 years took place in the United States—gun control policy seems to be at a halt. The NRA holds that individuals should have the right to bear arms, as mentioned in the Second Amendment. Some of the more militant members of the NRA believe that absolutely everyone should be able to bear arms without regulation, and those beliefs have translated into lobbying that makes gun control more difficult to enact.

While corporations are not allowed to directly fund any political campaign, political action committees (PACs) make it possible for corporations to ultimately foot the bill for many politicians to end up in offices. Corporations are allowed to fund many interest groups. This loophole allows them to affect many policies that ultimately mean that common people have to pay for the damages. Because corporate funding for interest groups influences so many political decisions, corporations have more power in Washington than even the politicians who hold the offices.

Although many interest groups are formed in order to take advantage of loopholes, other interest groups are still loyal to the ideal that they should be advocating for people whose voices cannot be heard and want to involve people in political action. Some of these interest groups include the American Civil Liberties Union (ACLU), the National Association for the Advancement of Colored People (NAACP), and the United States Women's Chamber of Commerce. Some of these interest groups, when they lack funding, may take more direct political action through protesting or civil disobedience. Though it is difficult to discern every interest group's motives, there are still groups that are committed to making political change for the better of their members.

In this section, we will discover the advantages and disadvantages of a two-party system in the United States, how interest groups interact with political parties, what methods interest groups utilize in order to influence political decisions, which interest groups are honest and which interest groups are fronts for corporate greed, and how to get involved with political parties and interest groups to make sure that citizens have their say in the democratic process.

POLITICAL PARTICIPATION +

Here in the United States, our Democracy allows us room to express various forms of dissent. However, not all forms of political participation are in the form of a demand. We will consider three umbrella categories of political participation. Conventional participation includes activities that are sanctioned by society as normal and appropriate. These include running for office, voting, working at a polling location, making a contribution to a campaign, or belonging to an activist group. Increasingly, the last option, belonging to an activist group, is becoming more and more unconventional.

Traditionally, unconventional participation includes legal activities that may be disruptive to business as usual. This includes marches, rallies, and the gathering of signatures to force a petition on the ballot. All of these methods are used regularly in order to fully recognize the will of the people.

Illegal participation would include any activity that, outside of the political sphere, would be considered illegal. This includes assassinations, terrorism, harassment, assault, vandalism, hacking, and theft. Depending on the basis of your understanding of conventional or unconventional levels of participation, one type may seem more rational than the other. For example, rational choice theorists propose that voting is irrational as there is no guarantee that your one vote will make a difference, while in some cases, these theorists may be in favor of unconventional strategies if the likelihood of a response from those in power is higher. Political thinkers like this believe that the cost of time taken to travel to a polling location is wasted time, and the energy used to educate yourself about the election is too much in comparison to the likelihood of your vote counting. This dynamic, often expressed among the American public, is called the paradox of participation.

OPEN SECRETS: POLITICS AND MONEY

Open Secrets (a project of Center for Responsive Politics) is a website that offers the behind the scenes information on the financial backing of corporations to candidates. This is commonly known as the "money trail." For decades the corporate interests have been strengthened with campaign contributions. This type of political participation is legal and widely used. However, some scholars believe that corporate power outweighs the power of the individual because many of us do not have the means to provide a corporation with $20,000 our financial contribution might be $35.

The amount doesn't symbolize the impact of their interest or the way in which the decision the candidate will and could make as an elected official. In 2010 the Citizens United versus the Federal Elections Commission (FEC) based on the premise that corporations were "people"—legal entities—and that their ability to fully participate in the political process was being stunted by caps on fundraising and media ads. The Supreme Court ruled in their favor—providing an enormous shift in how political campaigns were intended to be.

With your friends and family visit the website www.opensecrets.org. There you will find information on some of today's leading candidates and elected officials. The information includes how much money they have raised and for what election. Open Secrets also provide a breakdown of each corporation.

After reviewing the information (preferably with friends and family), discuss the potential links between the elected official or candidate—speculate on the corporation's interest and their economic and political backing of each person.

- Why would they give them money? What do you think they hope will happen?
- What corporations provided campaign contributions for each candidate?
- What major political issues are these corporations interested?

INTEREST GROUPS—EXPLORING SPECTRUMS OF INFLUENCE

Interest groups are defined by affinity and likeness of experience or opinion on political matters and strategies for governance. Some interest groups, like Mothers Against Drunk Driving (MADD) are groups that bring a higher awareness to issues impacted average people. Drunk driving has been a major social problem in the United States. With the advocacy, lobbying efforts, and public awareness campaigns, MADD has co-authored hundreds of new laws and strengthened the knowledge and response to alcohol abuse and vehicular irresponsibility.

Among the established organizations that work to increase the impact of citizen voices in the political process is the American Legislative Exchange Council. There is a certain subset of issues and perspectives that this group focuses on. Their charge is to develop "model" policies that lawmakers can utilize in their cities, states, and federally. As you learn about interest groups and the various ways that they impact politics, think back to the American Political Ideologies (Part Three) and the understanding associated with each type of political thinker.

ALEC—THE AMERICAN LEGISLATIVE EXCHANGE COUNCIL

According to their website, ALEC or the "American Legislative Exchange Council (ALEC) is a 501(c)(3) non-profit organization. It provides a constructive forum for state legislators and private sector leaders to discuss and exchange practical, state-level public policy issues.

The potential solutions discussed at ALEC focus on free markets, limited government and constitutional division of powers between the federal and state governments."

You will come to find that the missions of both organizations are easy to understand. So let's unpack it a bit. In the mission statement, they openly admit to bringing leaders from corporations together with elected officials to craft policy on the statewide level. Their hope is to create model legislation to be used in a variety of states where there is legislative will or backing from the public. Strategy in politics is everything. The direction, the ideology that influences that direction as well as the intended and unintended consequences.

Their strategy includes remaining true to three clear notions of American political thought: free markets, limited government, and the division of power between states and the national government. What does this mean? Nowhere in the mission statement does the organization imply or consider the will of the people may be important to include when making decisions on how our communities will change in the future.

For example, Senate Bill SB 1070 ("Support Our Law Enforcement and Safe Neighborhoods Act") was passed in Arizona, which legalized racial profiling against individuals who appeared to "look like an immigrant." In Arizona, many immigrants come from Latin American countries, but not all of them. This bill gave the police enforcement official's carte blanche to harass and demand papers from any brown person and, if caught, they will be incarcerated or deported.

A person's physical characteristics are legally the primary measurement of criminality in Arizona regarding this bill. ALEC helped created this bill and has worked with legislatures across the nation to replicate it. Each bill that ALEC writes is in partnership with legislators and corporations that have a vested interest in the outcome of the change in law. The Corrections Corporation of America was written with Arizona State Senator Russell Pearce at their 2009 Annual Conference.

Questions to consider: What are the benefits and disadvantages of having a bill like SB 1070? Is undocumented immigration a real criminal justice threat or an unmanaged administrative process? Why do you think immigration has become criminalized?

In what ways can the corporations that support the SB 1070 bill benefit? News reports have revealed that prison companies helped write part of the SB 1070 bill with hopes of increasing their business by increasing populations in private prisons? Is this just? Is this an acceptable way to influence legislation? What does this time of political change say about the culture within the United States?

POLITICAL PARTIES

The two parties that have been gaining the most political traction for the better part of two decades have been the Democrats and the Republicans. In actuality, this two-party system has gone through a number of iterations. When the United States was first establishing independence, there was a hope that the nation would be able to self-govern without bipartisanship in place. Two parties emerged when the Secretary of the Treasury, Alexander Hamilton, and James Madison found that their political philosophies differed too intensely to be a coincidence. These differences gave birth to the Federalist and Democratic-Republican parties during the 1797 election.

In order to ensure that citizens were having their opinions fairly considered by their elected officials, the party system became a means of categorizing politicians and voters, essentially working as a guide for how to cast a vote about specific topics or offices.

The only time in American history that this two-party system was actively avoided was during the period between 1817 and 1825 during former President Monroe's administration immediately after the War of 1812. The nation was interested in maintaining a unified outlook and the Federalist Party had already become disbanded, leaving room for the Democratic-Republican Party to hold dominance in office.

However, even during this presumed stalemate in competition between parties, there was still tension within the Democratic-Republican Party that resulted in the new National Republicans being formed when the Democratic-Republican Party fell apart. Soon afterward, the Whig Party established itself as opposition against the new Democratic Party.

Originally serving as the conservative party, the Democratic Party did not become a champion for liberal issues such as welfare, civil rights, reproductive rights, and environmental issues until President Franklin Delano Roosevelt started the programs that would be known as the New Deal. In effect from 1933 to 1936, the New Deal was enacted in response to the Great Depression. Put into place to neutralize the deep economic downturn that took place during the Depression, it also served to change the discourse that Americans would use to describe their political leanings.

The voters who supported the New Deal were considered "liberals," while those who were opposed were labeled "conservatives." The way that these political parties have been sold is by portraying the parties as two characters in a movie who do not agree with each other but have learned to make their living arrangements work while they have to share the space. What this narrative does is ignore that these roommates have friends who like to crash in their living room, often have advice when the two feud, share expenses, and, for all intents and purposes, essentially share a house.

THE DEMOCRATIC USE OF POLITICAL PARTIES

Many political scientists believe that political parties provide an avenue for average citizens to engage in the political process. When a citizen is inspired to lead, the party structure can also provide support for candidates to run for office.

When there is dissent against the current candidate in office, political parties can be used as a galvanizing body to get people involved in the process of addressing grievances toward their leadership.

Depending on the affiliation of the party, an organization can help individuals who are members of that organization run as a candidate to protect their rights of free expression and civil liberties. When there is competition among candidates in the same party, there is generally a party primary where members of each party can vote for the candidate they wish to represent them. A party structure allows its members to hold one another accountable to a platform of issues and beliefs about the "correct" solution to problems. As leaders in American politics, parties serve as a screening body for candidates and as a source of social and cultural politicization. Political parties have a vested interest in educating the public by sharing their narrative on a variety of issues. This could come in the form of public meetings, polls, debates, and so forth. The role of the party varies as it is utilized across the country.

All states have party organizations (at minimum Republican and Democratic) that operate state level party business. This is important to maintain local and regional support and to keep citizens connected with one of the political parties. Party identification happens when a person relates to an entity through intellectual and emotional connections generally related to the platform presented.

OVERVIEW OF POLITICAL CAMPAIGNS IN OUR DEMOCRACY

Throughout the history of America's Democracy, campaigns have been an important process for everyone involved. The politicians who are vying for the public's vote find that the campaign trail serves as a perfect preview for how hard they are going to work during their term if they win. If they lose, then it is a hard lesson learned and perhaps a walk of shame if the campaign was a complete embarrassment.

For voters, there is a hope that they will have an opportunity to finally believe in their elected officials. The first time someone votes is considered a rite of passage. It is proof that they have reached a level of responsibility and maturity where their political autonomy has direction and purpose.

Campaigns offer the possibility of reform and political change for those who believe in the system and another round of entertainment for people who see the game that is being played for what it is: politics.

The means by which campaigns have been run obviously change as methods to share information evolve. Print and public appearances have been a political favorite for centuries, if only because of the simplicity of knowing that a politician's statements can be edited for quality when in print and knowing that when a good impression is made to the public, there is a better chance of being considered a viable, honest candidate. The truth behind these appearances and statements may not necessarily persist when the person wins the election, but they can certainly present the illusion of sincerity long enough to win.

For the first time in political history, 21st century candidates have the opportunity to use the Internet as a primary campaign tool. The Internet has made it possible to more easily extend political promises, ideological beliefs, propaganda, and smear campaigns against opponents. The Internet also allows citizens to more readily research candidates and learn more about their political leanings to ensure that they are making responsible voting decisions. Despite the opportunities that the Internet affords people to educate themselves, are people more informed about campaigns?

Campaigns during the 21st century have certainly seen a difference in coverage. The reception to this coverage has also shifted over the course of history. The first televised presidential debate was in 1960, and because of this, there was a shift in how people thought about politics. Appearance and likability became a notable trait. Americans were able to watch the candidates answer questions under pressure, which affected their decision making process when voting. Now, learning about a candidate's beliefs and past is a simple Google search away. Debates are live-streamed on YouTube, and there are more options for voters to educate themselves. The voters who are now coming of age have grown up with technology and are able to learn about candidates through their social media profiles. The exposure to these politicians has caused a collective cognitive dissonance, if only because the promises that are made during the political campaigns often clash both with the politicians' pasts and, as it often turns out, their future actions.

Websites like WikiLeaks and FactCheck.org allow people to access confidential government documents about "a gray area" issues and to fact-check a candidate's claims during campaigns. As a result, there is a generalized distrust of government and a stronger reliance on self-governance and grassroots efforts.

Ultimately, even politicians are not welcome to secrets during the Information Age, no matter how much they try to hide their public snafus and problematic beliefs from the public, especially during campaigns. Politicians are aware that their constituents agree with their politics simply because they seem like the lesser of two evils. Although there has been no real climate of self-accountability, the public still demands that politicians take responsibility for their actions and their statements during their campaigns. When there is a hint that a specific politician is not being honest, the polls and election results start to reflect that fact. Although George W. Bush was able to manipulate the system during the 2000 presidential election, the public has learned to pay closer attention during elections in the 21st century.

The change in demographics in just the last 20 years has affected what promises politicians will make about abortion, immigration, economic reform, education, and other social and fiscal issues. Focus has shifted from promises of future action to the candidates' track records in deciding who is least likely to jump off of the political platforms they built in favor of personal interests. People who were involved in President Obama's grassroots campaign movement during the 2008 presidential campaign understood that, by 2012, he was not the perfect candidate, but at least he was not Mitt Romney. Such acceptance of the less than ideal candidate has emerged as part of the new political discourse and, in the last 15 years, has become a political norm. In this section, we will focus on how campaigns have changed over the course of American history, what methods candidates use to win campaigns, how citizens respond to these methods, and how we can use the tools that are available to us in order to make responsible, well-informed decisions.

CAMPAIGN RULES

National campaigns have a specific set of rules that candidates and counties are meant to follow, under the auspices of giving the voter a fair choice between the candidates. These rules have been in the Constitution since the "Founding Fathers" first decided to have democratic elections and have since gone through a number of changes. Most notably, the Fourteenth Amendment, which gave former slaves and their descendants the right to vote, and the Nineteenth Amendment, which allowed women the right to vote. The 13th amendment abolished slavery unless it was used as punishment for a crime, which gave room for the 14th amendment to exist.

These amendments, and others, certainly made it possible for a larger group of people to have an opinion about what candidates would be representing them and making laws that would affect their livelihoods. There are still many more laws that need to be put into place to protect these citizens from being marginalized at voting booths and to make sure that their voices are heard accurately.

While there are a fair number of loopholes that are often used to work around these regulations, the rules are meant to offer transparency to the government and make it easier for the voter to make a decision about who they want representing their ideologies in the White House. Some of these rules are particularly important because they offer full disclosure to the public regarding where campaign funds stem from and limits corporations from making direct contributions for personal gain when the candidate wins. Instead, they are required to make their contributions to PACs, which then distribute the funds to a campaign. However, many of these PACs are not necessarily subtle about which corporations are funding them, as there are some that are called AT&T Inc. and Lockheed Martin, two of the largest corporations in the world. There are also rules that protect against a presidential candidate having more than two terms in office and allow people to vote whether or not they pay poll taxes. The next step is to ensure that, while these people have the national right to vote according to the Constitution, that they are not denied the right to vote because of county laws or gross misconduct, as seen in the 2000 elections.

STATEWIDE BALLOT INITIATIVES IN CALIFORNIA

California is one of 24 states that allows statewide ballot initiatives to be distributed by the public and included for voting consideration. Initiatives come in two forms: They can come from the legislative branch for the public's vote on a public ballot initiative. This initiative system allows California voters to have input in what new California Constitutional rights and laws are passed that will affect their living conditions in crucial ways. Initiative is one of the few ways that the democratic process is actually working for American citizens and allowing them to have a role in how laws are formulated.

The steps to create an initiative are quite simple, but are numerous. They span from the first step of making sure to properly draft the proposed law and collecting 25 electors' signatures; paying a $200 fee to submit the draft to the Attorney General, which will then be refunded should the initiative proposal qualify for the ballot within two years; to formatting the petition and collecting signatures from California citizens at least 131 days before the next statewide election. Once the signatures are verified and, if the petition passes signature verification, the proposed law is submitted to the ballot for the general election. After that, the natural order of elections will determine whether or not the initiative will be signed into law.

The main drawback to the current initiative system is that, oftentimes, there is not enough information about any given initiative. They rely on people walking around and collecting signatures after giving a brief summary of what the initiative is hoping to accomplish. However, with the rise of the Internet and smartphones, it is a lot easier to overcome this particular issue, since it is possible to research the issues of any given petition at a moment's notice. The initiative process is one of the few ways that the American citizen can have a direct effect on how laws are made and it is important that we become involved in how those laws turn out in the elections so that we cannot be caught off-guard by new changes that we did not approve.

OAKLAND, CALIFORNIA ELECTIONS

What is Rank Choice Voting?

The local Oakland government is in desperate need of a revamp. There have been certain council members who, despite the four-year staggered terms that every council member must serve, have been on the city council for as long as ten or twenty years. During that time, their districts have not seen a drop in criminal activity or, more notably in the recent past, a decrease in police brutality. This particular fact has been a thorn in Oakland residents' sides for decades and has bred a general malcontent for the police and the Oakland government. The most recent protests that took place during the Occupy movement, which resulted in many police raids against peaceful protesters threatened Mayor Jean Quan's term, with many residents insisting that she be recalled. However, she was able to hold onto her office for the remainder of her term and even win a second term in office, thanks in part to a new voting system.

In 2012, Oakland decided to use a new voting method called ranked-choice voting. This method allows voters to rank their candidates based on preference, which eliminates the need for run-off elections where there is a subsequent vote to decide between the candidates who received the highest and second-highest number of votes in any given election. Ranked-choice voting gives the voters an option to rank three candidates in order of preference. Oakland uses this particular method of voting to elect the Mayor, City Council members, City Attorney, City Auditor, and School Directors.

The 2000 Election

In the 2000 national elections, the main contenders were George W. Bush on the Republican ticket and Al Gore on the Democratic ticket. The campaign leading up to Election Day was fierce as each candidate worked to stand proudly on their political platforms while trying to kick the support beams out from under the opposing candidate's platform. Al Gore was working on his past experience as a Vice President under President Clinton. President George W. Bush was relying heavily on nepotism.

The media was unfair and biased, as usual. The news media covered Al Gore in a tone that made him look megalomaniacal, claiming that he'd "invented the Internet" and discovered the Love Canal, a famous toxic-waste dumpsite. These media tricks worked against Gore in a major way, working in Bush's favor during the campaign. During Election Day, many Democrats were still holding onto hope that Gore would win while Republicans were fairly certain that Bush was guaranteed to be the next President. While pundits regularly poked fun at the intelligence of the then-candidate George W. Bush, his family's legacy allowed him to remain in the President's seat longer than earned.

It was the Florida ballots and the Supreme Court that would be the deciding factor during the elections. Florida was that year's swing state for the presidential election. Coincidentally, Jeb Bush, George W. Bush's younger brother, was the governor of Florida from 1999 to 2007. The swing state essentially breaks any ties that would take place during an election, helping to swing the vote toward one candidate or another. Controversy arose when various counties came under fire because it was discovered that many of the voting machines in lower-income counties had higher spoilage rates compared to more affluent counties. Some of the voting machines did not register that a voter made a selection for the presidential option. There were also rumors that people were essentially forced to wait for hours on Voting Day because of supposed registration errors, which undoubtedly affected how many people were allowed to vote.

By the time the votes were counted, Bush was coming out in the lead in the election. Al Gore quickly requested a recount of four of the more heavily Democrat counties. This debate over the recount and the inclusion of ballots would go on to become a Supreme Court case, *Bush v. Gore*. The recount was deemed unconstitutional by the Supreme Court in December 2000, and Bush became the 43rd President of the United States. There is still heavy debate about which candidate could have won if the recount had been allowed. The court intervention prevented the votes from being included in the 2000 Presidential election.

AN OVERVIEW OF THE AMERICAN ELECTION SYSTEM

Elections give citizens a voice in their government in the most fundamental way: by deciding who governs.

Elections help ensure that power passes in a peaceful, orderly manner from citizens to their elected representatives—and from one elected official to their successor. The U.S. Constitution gives certain powers to the national (or "federal") government and reserves others for the individual states and the people. In many countries, national governments set education and health policies, but in the United States, the 50 states have primary responsibility in these areas. National defense and foreign policy are examples of federal responsibility. The Constitution requires that each state have a republican form of government. It forbids states from violating certain specified rights (e.g., "No State shall…deprive any person of life, liberty, or property, without due process of law; nor deny to any person within its jurisdiction the equal protection of the laws."). But states otherwise retain considerable power. The American system can appear complicated, but it ensures that voters have a voice at all levels of government.

When George Washington was elected as the first president in 1789, only 6% of the U.S. population could vote. In most of the original 13 states, only landowning men over the age of 21 had the right to vote. Today, the U.S. Constitution guarantees that all U.S. citizens over the age of 18 can vote in federal (national), state, and local elections.

The U.S. Constitution sets the requirements for holding federal office, but each of the 50 states has its own Constitution and its own rules for state offices. For example, governors in most states serve four-year terms, but in other states, the governor is elected for only two years. Voters in some states elect judges, while in others, judges are appointed to office. States and localities elect thousands of public officials—from governors and state legislators to school board members and even dogcatchers. The only elected federal officials are the president and vice president and members of Congress—the 435 members of the U.S. House of Representatives and the 100 senators.

The U.S. Constitution establishes the requirements for holding an elected federal office. To serve as president, one must be a natural-born citizen of the United States, at least 35 years old, and a resident of the United States for at least 14 years. A vice president must meet the same criteria. Under the 12th Amendment to the U.S. Constitution, the vice president cannot have served two terms as president. Candidates for the U.S. House of Representatives must be at least 25 years old, have been U.S. citizens for seven years, and be legal residents of the state they seek to represent in Congress. U.S. Senate candidates must be at least 30, U.S. citizens for nine years, and legal residents of the state they wish to represent.

Elections for federal office are held in even-numbered years. The presidential election is held every four years and takes place on the Tuesday after the first Monday in November. Elections for all 435 seats in the U.S. House of Representatives are held every two years. U.S. senators serve six-year terms that are staggered so that one-third (or one-third plus one) of the 100 Senate seats come up for election every two years. If a senator dies or becomes incapacitated while in office, a special election can be held in an odd-numbered year or in the next even-numbered year. The newly elected senator serves until the end of the original senator's term. In some states, the governor appoints someone to serve the remainder of the original term.

After George Washington, the first president declined to run for a third term, and many Americans believed that two terms in office were enough for any president. None of Washington's successors sought a third term until 1940, when, at a time marked by the Great Depression and World War II, Franklin D. Roosevelt sought, and won, a third presidential term. He won a fourth term in 1944 and died in office in 1945. Some people thought that was too long for one person to hold presidential power. So in 1951, the 22nd Amendment to the U.S. Constitution was ratified, which prohibits anyone from being elected president of the United States more than twice.

There are no term limits for members of Congress. Term limits, if any, for state and local officials are spelled out in state constitutions and local ordinances. The two chambers of the U.S. Congress, the House of Representatives and the Senate have nearly equal powers, but their means of getting elected are quite different. The Founders of the American Republic intended members of the House of Representatives to be close to the public, reflecting the public's wishes and ambitions. Therefore, the Founders designed the House to be relatively large to accommodate many members from small legislative districts and to have frequent elections (every two years).

Each of the 50 states is entitled to one seat in the House, with additional seats allocated according to population. Alaska, for example, has a very small population and therefore has only one U.S. representative. California, the most populous state, has 55. Every 10 years the U.S. Census is taken, and House seats are reallocated among the states based on the new population figures. Each state draws the boundaries of its congressional districts. States have considerable latitude in how they do this, so long as the number of citizens in each district is as close to equal as possible. Unsurprisingly, when one party controls the state government, it tries to draw the boundaries to the benefit of its own congressional candidates. The Senate was designed for its members to represent larger constituencies—an entire state—and to provide equal representation for each state, regardless of population. Thus, small states possess as much influence (two senators) as large states in the Senate.

The two chambers of the U.S. Congress, the House of Representatives and the Senate, have nearly equal powers, but their means of election are quite different.

The drafters of the U.S. Constitution did not envision political parties. But, as voting rights broadened and the nation expanded westward, political parties emerged. Two major parties—Democrats and Whigs—became firmly established and powerful by the 1830s. Today, the Republican and Democratic parties dominate the political process—both of them heirs to predecessor parties from the 18th and 19th centuries. With rare exceptions, members of the two major parties control the presidency, the Congress, the governorships and the state legislatures. Every president since 1852 has been either a Republican or a Democrat.

Rarely do any of the 50 states elect a governor who is not a Democrat or a Republican. And the number of independent or third-party members of Congress or of state legislatures is extremely low. Why aren't there more small parties? Many political experts point to America's "first past the post" elections, in which the candidate with the most votes wins, even if they receive less than a majority of the votes cast. In countries that instead award legislative seats based on the proportion of votes a given party receives, there is more incentive for small parties to form and compete. In the U.S. system, a party can win a seat only if its candidate gets the most votes. That makes it difficult for small political parties to win elections.

In recent decades, increasing numbers of American voters call themselves politically "independent" or affiliated with no party. Yet opinion polls suggest that most independents lean toward either the Republican or Democratic Party. Some do belong to smaller political parties. Regardless of party affiliation—or lack thereof—all Americans age 18 and older are allowed to vote in local, state, and presidential elections. How does the two-party system represent the beliefs of Americans who affiliate with neither party? Sometimes Americans feel that neither major party advances their preferred policies and beliefs. One strategy they may pursue is to form a new party for the purpose of demonstrating the popularity of their ideas. One famous example occurred in 1892 when dissatisfied Americans formed the Populist Party. Its platform called for a graduated income tax, direct election of senators, and an eight-hour workday. The Populists never captured the presidency, but the big parties noticed their new competitor's growing popularity. The Democrats and Republicans began to adopt many of the Populists' ideas, and in time the ideas became the law of the land.

During the summer of a presidential election year, the Republicans and Democrats each hold a national convention where they adopt a "platform" of policies and nominate their party's candidates for president and vice president. Today, a simple majority of delegates' votes is needed to capture the nomination. In earlier times, the conventions were exciting, with outcomes uncertain and candidates rising and falling with each ballot. Sometimes negotiations were held in "smoke-filled" hotel rooms, where cigarette and cigar-smoking party leaders cut deals to secure their preferred candidate the required delegate votes. Today the process is more transparent, and for about the last 60 years, each party's presidential nominee was known before its convention began. Each state (plus the District of Columbia and several U.S. territories) is allotted a number of delegates—typically determined by the state's population but adjusted by a formula that awards bonuses for factors like whether a state voted for the party's candidate in the last presidential election. Most delegates are "pledged" to support a particular candidate, at least on the first ballot, and no convention has required more than one ballot to nominate its presidential candidate for many years.

Primary elections and caucuses differ in how they are organized and who participates. And rates of participation differ widely. Primaries: State governments fund and conduct primary elections much as they would any election: Voters go to a polling place, vote, and leave. Voting is anonymous and quickly accomplished. Some states hold "closed" primaries in which only declared party members could participate. For example, only registered Democrats can vote in a closed Democratic primary. In an open primary, all voters can participate, regardless of their party affiliation or lack of affiliation. Caucuses: State political parties organize caucuses in which faithful party members speak openly on behalf of the candidates they support for the party nomination. They are communal events in which participants vote publicly. Caucuses tend to favor candidates who have dedicated and organized supporters who can use the caucus to elect convention delegates pledged to their favored presidential candidate. Caucus participants also identify and prioritize issues they want to include in the state or national party platform. Participation in a caucus requires a high level of political engagement and time. Consequently, caucuses tend to attract fewer participants than primaries.

Historically, only a few states held presidential primaries or caucuses. But the trend has been toward greater voter participation in the presidential nomination process. The number of states holding primaries or caucuses started increasing in the 1970s. Today all 50 states and the District of Columbia have either presidential primaries or caucuses. States parties choose whether they want to hold a primary or a caucus, and some states have switched from one format to the other over time. Some states have both primaries and caucuses. For example, in Alaska and Nebraska, Republicans hold primaries while Democrats convene caucuses. In Kentucky, Democrats hold a primary and Republicans a caucus.

For many years, Iowa has held the first caucuses, generally in January or early February of the presidential election year, and New Hampshire the first primary, a short time later. Because these and other early contests frequently establish which candidates lack enough support to contend seriously for the presidency, candidates expend great effort in these early states, addressing their needs and interests and organizing campaigns within even smaller states, spending money on staff, media, and hotels. As a result, more and more states schedule their primaries and caucuses in the winter months. Many states hold their events on the same day. The major parties frequently tweak the rules in ways they hope will produce the strongest possible candidate. For example, in 2016, the Republicans will allow states that hold their primaries after March 15 to award their delegates "winner-take-all," so that the candidate who earns the most votes—even if it's only, say, 25% of the votes in an eight-candidate field—will capture all that state's delegates. A major outcome of the proliferation and acceleration of primaries and caucuses is that the nominees of the major parties are known before the national party conventions are held in late summer. This has diminished the importance of the national nominating conventions, which have become largely ceremonial events.

If the presidential candidates are selected through the primaries and caucuses, why do the two major political parties still hold national nominating conventions? It's because the conventions give each party the opportunity to promote its nominees and define its differences with the opposition. The nominating conventions are widely televised and mark the start of the national presidential campaigns. Americans still watch the nominating conventions to hear speeches by party leaders and nominees, the choice of the nominee's vice presidential candidate (sometimes not announced until the convention), the roll call of delegate votes by the state delegations, and the ratification of the party "platform" (the document that spells out each party's positions on the issues).

After the nationwide presidential election is held in November, the Electoral College meets in December. In most states, electors cast their votes based on how the majority of voters in their state voted. The electors vote in their states on December 15, and Congress officially counts the results in January. Each state has a number of electors equal to the number of its members in the U.S. House of Representatives—determined by a census of the state's population, plus its two senators. The District of Columbia, which is not a state and has no voting representation in Congress, has three Electoral College votes. There are 538 electors in the Electoral College; 270 electoral votes are needed to win the presidential election. Most states award electoral votes on a winner-take-all basis. The presidential ticket that gets the most citizens' votes receives all that state's electoral votes.

It's in the Constitution, but it isn't easy to amend the Constitution. The Electoral College system also reinforces the two-party system, which means neither of the two major parties is likely to advocate a change. But there are other reasons for retaining the Electoral College. Many Americans like how the Electoral College system forces presidential candidates to campaign widely—even in smaller states whose residents might not otherwise have the chance to see candidates up close. And because presidential candidates cannot garner enough electoral votes by focusing on a single state or region, they learn about and address issues of interest to voters in all parts of the country. As a consequence, the Electoral College system influences how presidential campaigns are conducted, which has important implications for the cost of running a presidential campaign.

Since 1976, candidates for president have been eligible to participate in a public financing system to pay for their campaigns. Until the 2000 elections, all candidates nominated for president participated in this system by accepting government funds in exchange for a promise not to spend more than a specified amount. However, this system has become increasingly unappealing to candidates because the imposed spending limit is considered too low—and less than the amount that major candidates can often raise from private sources. Consequently, some recent presidential candidates have opted out of public funding and instead raised money to fund their campaigns.

In 2010, the Supreme Court ruled that political spending is a form of speech and thus protected by the First Amendment to the U.S. Constitution. As a result, since 2010, candidates can spend an unlimited amount of their own money to fund their campaigns. The ruling also gave greater leeway to "PACs", which are formed when individuals, businesses and interest groups pool their money and donate it to support specific ideas, candidates, ballot initiatives or legislation. According to federal law, an organization becomes a PAC when it receives or spends more than $2,600 for the purpose of influencing a federal election. States have their own laws governing when an organization becomes a PAC. Because they are independent of a candidate's official fundraising committee, PACs are not subject to the same regulations—even though they must register with the Federal Election Commission—but they are limited in how closely they can coordinate with candidates. For example, a PAC cannot contribute more than $5,000 directly to a candidate's election committee, but it can spend an unlimited amount of money to run ads that advocate or oppose a specific candidate's views.

Most U.S. election results are not particularly close, but occasionally there are races with a very small margin of victory or races in which the outcome is contested, and votes are recounted. This happened in parts of Florida during the 2000 U.S. presidential election—the closest in U.S. history. That race forced many Americans to consider the myriad administrative tasks surrounding their elections for the first time. The U.S. Constitution gives citizens age 18 and above the right to vote. There is no national list of eligible voters, so localities create them by requiring citizens to register as voters. This is to prevent fraud. In the past, selective registration procedures were used to discourage some citizens—most notably, African Americans in the South—from voting. Today, the Voting Rights Act prohibits these discriminatory practices. Each state establishes its own registration requirements. Citizens who move are required to re-register at their new place of residence. At times, states have made registration easier, and at other times, they have tightened the requirements. In 1993, the National Voter Registration Act made it possible for citizens to register to vote when they renew their state-issued driver's license. Some states allow voters to register on Election Day. Recently, however, some states have passed laws that require government-issued identification or eliminate registration on Election Day.

One of the important lessons of the extremely close 2000 presidential election was that the election administration, balloting and vote-counting challenges encountered in Florida could have occurred almost anywhere in the United States. Several studies were commissioned, and a variety of panels heard expert witnesses and took testimony about the need for reform. In 2002, Congress passed the Help America Vote Act to address the problems of the 2000 election and anticipate new ones. First, the federal government funded state and local efforts to replace outdated punch-card and lever voting machines. Second, it established the Election Assistance Commission to afford local election technical assistance and to help local officials establish voting device standards. The commission studies voting machine and ballot design, registration and provisional voting methods, deterring fraud, procedures for recruiting and training poll workers, and voter education programs. The Help America Vote Act marks a significant expansion of the federal government's role in a matter traditionally left to localities. But the reforms introduced have helped restore faith in the U.S. election process.

Some content from: https://publications.america.gov/wp-content/uploads/sites/8/2016/05/Elections-USA_In-Brief-Series_English_Hi-Res.pdf

IMPORTANT FACTS AND TERMS

Bipartisan Campaign Reform Act (BCRA): The Bipartisan Campaign Reform Act of 2002 amended the FECA of 1971 and prevents federal elections from using non-federal funds. This Act also regulates how much any federal or non-federal candidate can fundraise for party committee, other candidates, and nonprofit organizations.

Benchmark poll: A poll that is often taken before a politician announces his or her candidacy for office. It is used to measure the citizens are likely to vote for that particular politician.

Exit poll: A poll that is often taken while or after voters leave a voting booth. It is used to get a gauge, but not necessarily predict, the outcome of a given election.

Bipartisanship: The political system in which two parties have majority power in the government. This often results in only two options for any given election.

Caucus: A meeting of supporters or members of a particular political candidate's campaign or party to discuss specific details of a campaign or political action.

Duverger's law: A theory proposed by Maurice Duverger that posits that a one-ballot voting method favors a two-party government system. This system allows for smaller parties to fuse together to form one larger party for party representation to help guarantee to win the election.

Electoral College: The official process that elects the President and the Vice President. There are 538 electors in the Electoral College, and a 270 majority vote is required in order to elect a President and Vice President. Since every President has a set number of electors, the citizens' vote allows the Electoral College to know which electors will be included in the Electoral College when they vote.

Federal Election Campaign Act (FECA): The Federal Election Campaign Act (FECA) of 1971 placed limits on how much a campaign could spend on media advertising, which was later repealed, and required campaigns to publicly disclose campaign expenditures. The FECA also laid the groundwork for PACs to separate funding channels.

Focus group: Primarily a marketing tool that started to be embraced in politics in the 1950s and 1960s, this tool allows politicians to better understand voters through controlled tests and polls where citizens give their opinions and ideas about specific issues. This particular tool changes the citizens' roles from responsible voters to political consumers and the politicians' roles from civil servants to political businessman.

Front loading: To concentrate expenditures to the beginning of a period, specifically a campaign.

General election: An election that involves all or most of the constituencies of a nation or a state.

Initiative: Initiatives are petitions concerning specific sociopolitical issues that can be presented on the voting ballot, effectively making it possible for people to influence what laws are made and enforced. Only twenty-four states allow initiatives in their voting process.

Libertarian: A political party that believes in the autonomy of the individual and businesses. Another political party that works better in theory, oftentimes, the Libertarian Party believes in minimum government and that citizens should be able to govern themselves.

McConnell v. FEC: A 2002 Supreme Court case that enacted the Bipartisan Campaign Reform Act (BCRA), which is meant to address loopholes that were present in the FECA.

Micro-targeting: Another technique similar to a marketing tool, micro-targeting is a political strategy of data mining a particular citizen group's interests to identify like individuals and predict their actions in order to better appeal to them during campaigns.

Minor party: Minor parties, also called "third parties," are the alternative to the two popular parties in a two-party system. Examples of minor parties in the United States include the Peace and Freedom Party, the Green Party, the Libertarian Party, and the Communist Party.

Motor Voter Act: Also known as the National Voter Registration Act of 1993 (NVRA), which requires state and federal elections to allow voters the opportunity to register to vote either when they apply for or renew their driver's license/identification card, by mail, or various state-provided locations. States are required to keep their voter rosters updated, including but not limited to when a voter has been convicted of a crime.

National party convention: Held in August of recent election years, the national party convention is a party's opportunity to announce its candidates and political platforms for the campaign trail. This particular process has been important in recent years because of the advent of media resources from television and the Internet.

Opinion poll: A poll that asks the general public's opinion of a particular issue or politician, then presents the results in a statistical format.

Party in government: The organized parties that individual members who serve in public office.

Party in the electorate: A member of a particular party who only votes for candidates of that same party.

Party organization: The structures and procedures a political party follows.

Party primary: The selection process that takes allows the citizens to vote on who will be put onto the official voting ballot during general elections.

Party unity: A sense of solidarity and commonality amongst a party's members, politicians, and candidates.

Primary: The selection process that takes allows the citizens to vote on who will be put onto the official voting ballot during general elections.

Recall: A process by which citizens are allowed to vote about having a political official removed from his or her office before the end of their term.

Referendum: Any measure that appears on a ballot. The two types are legislative referenda, which is when the Legislature proposes a measure to the public on a ballot, and popular referenda, which is a measure that was put through the citizen petition process to appear on the ballot.

Soft money: Non-federal funds that are not for any particular candidate and, therefore, negate any regulations that may be handed down from the FEC.

Voter registration: The process by which a citizen enters his or her name into the central registry to ensure that they are able to vote during elections.

Voter turnout: The statistical amount of how many people went out to vote during any given election period.

CHAPTER FIVE

Social and Economic Inequalities in The U.S.

The democracy we have been gifted with today has come at a price. The price has been the people lives and our time. Essentially thousands of days where American citizens and residents are working together and oftentimes against one another. Although I'd like to think that an engaged citizenry would afford equality as a central theme for their participation in the political process. Sadly, this is not true. Not all people believe that equity, justice, and freedom mean the same thing. This is the difficult part. The concept of people power has two dimensions—the first being the rights of the people that are expressed in the Constitution and the organizing efforts among the citizens to maintain and expand the interpretation of fairness, power, and dissemination of resources. The second dimension of people power is the innate will to survive and live just lives. This is exhibited in our development and practice of personal and political agency. Personal agency is your individual will to lead your own life by a particular set of values. Political agency is your ability and interest in putting those values to work for a common goal or good will.

We are motivated by our or other's personal experiences in relationship to the government and other systems. This helps us shape our perspective what strategy we will use to create change in our political system.

SOCIAL AND ECONOMIC INEQUITIES

Many of you will remember the 2008 financial crisis that resulted in bank failures and the foreclosure of homes for millions of families across the country. The financial product and the people who sold sub-prime loans created a bubble in the market and it burst. Just like it did during the Great Depression. The main difference is that the wealth of our nation isn't spread out like it used to be.

There was a time when the wealth gap wasn't as large. Speculatively, we could say that it is a positive thing without critically examining the use of capitalism as a way to organize and govern our economic habits. Why do we maintain this gap? Can we organize our system differently so we cannot profit off the plight of other people?

So—what happened with the 2008 crash? Because the loaning system was so broken, the government issued a Capital Purchase Program that would prop up capital and support banks into lending to individuals again. Now because the wealth is so concentrated into the top 10% to 15% of Americans, when the banks and insurance companies failed us we felt it, but not all of us. Some of us lost our homes while others just read about it on the news. Why such a stark difference even among neighbors? What are the structures within our government that are set to protect American consumer and economic interests?

https://usafacts.org/data/topics/people-society/poverty/

Katznelson, Kesselman, and Draper (2009) said it best, "when key sectors of the private economy fail spectacularly, as the automobile industry recently has, government has little choice but to step in to shepherd them back to self-sustaining health" (p. 10). This recent example of the imbalance in the distribution of wealth isn't a new story in the American narrative. Unfortunately, because there has always been a leisure class and a working class within our capitalist system, the haves and the have-nots is a binary that is strong in American politics.

Class differences are often exacerbated in the media during election years. The reporting on unemployment rates and the income gap between men and women become hot topics for pundits and politicians to discuss. Both issues speak to a larger more philosophical question of structural inequality in the American system of government and the structural inequality creates the conditions for injustice to occur right under our noses. What makes this level of inequality structural is that it is written into the system. This means that, in many ways, the system is designed to promote inequality. Some people in the system realized this and, because some social and economic inequalities are glaringly obvious, regulatory agencies are meant to not only protect citizens from harm, but also to create a balance of opportunity and access.

SOCIAL CONTROLS ON COMMUNICATION

Much of the economic and domestic policy developed in the United States is in response to a problem that arises in the public or private spheres. These responses tend to be geared toward the most conservative change for individuals and a more progressive response for corporations. We see this within cities like Oakland, California where major corporations are looking to relocate and a tax break is offered to them to relocate. This is essentially relocation assistance for corporations. Individuals rarely, if at all, get this benefit.

Some of this can be negated with limitations in understanding of the problem, but most of the policies are intended to have a positive impact for the people or the corporate or government interests. In this section you would be exposed to a brief history of economic and social regulation in this country through the development and utility of a major regulatory agency, the Federal Communications Commission (FCC), and the use of regulation and deregulation in managing economic and human needs.

The FCC "regulates interstate and international communications by radio, television, wire, satellite and cable in all 50 states, the District of Columbia and U.S. territories." Issues handled by the FCC include a wide array of concerns that include public safety and access. Rulemaking occurs within the FCC that mandates Congress to give them the authority to propose statutes. Rulemaking can occur in three different ways.

Congress can identify a rule or begin the rulemaking process to fully understand a problem. The FCC, as a regulatory agency, can identify a problem that has a negative impact on consumers of communication technology. Because we have a democracy, most regulatory agencies have a petitioning process to influence the rulemaking that the body presides over. The public can petition this agency to modify or rescind a rule that they may disagree with and want altered for the public good.

The FCC has been under pressure recently as the issue of net neutrality has been a buzzword in many tech circles. Net neutrality is one of those hot topic issues. The questions posed here are on the basis of who gets to decide what is available to consumers, the people or the corporations. Especially if the technology offered or withheld is a benefit to the common good and, because it is so widely accepted as an important aspect in our capitalist democracy, a right that everyone should have access to. For example, "In 2007 the American public discovered that Comcast, the nation's largest cable provider, was blocking several basic, legal Internet technologies enabling peer-to-peer transactions. In response to complaints, the FCC ordered Comcast to stop. Comcast appealed to the D.C. Circuit, and that court ruled in 2010 that the FCC didn't have the jurisdiction to act." Decisions made by corporations affect our daily lives. The roles of regulatory agencies are meant to strengthen democracy and rotate the shift of power to balance the needs of the people with those in private or public power.

CORPORATE PERSONHOOD

The question of regulation sits at the ideological base of American politics. The impact of laissez faire capitalism and the fiscally conservative drive to maintain a "free market" has created economic growth and economic devastation. This devastation rarely reached the corporations that caused the economic plight and it most definitely impacted most American citizens and residents. The Great Depression, the bank bailouts, and the savings and loans scandals are just a few examples of a lack of government regulation leaving corporations and big banks in charge of the economy and allowing citizens to suffer from irresponsible decision making. Why is this right or wrong?

In recent decades, we've seen corporations taking the big pay outs and leaving the people behind to pay for their collective loses. A major win for big business, to secure this reality for the next generation, came down with a Supreme Court decision in 1886. Arguably, this case began the initial debate on corporate personhood. Some political scientists speculate that the leaders of corporations knew early on the real benefit of being in the United States was to have the benefit of the expressed protections in the Constitution.

The 14th Amendment is meant to provide citizens of the United States equal protection under the law regardless of the state they are in. Corporations, like the South Pacific Railroad Company, interpreted this equal protection to mean that they couldn't be taxed in more than one state, even if they were doing business nationally. The *Santa Clara County v. Southern Pacific Railroad Company* decision started with regional counties concerned about the tax revenue they were missing out on by the Southern Pacific Railroad Company not pay taxes. This interpretation led to future cases where the citizenships rights of people were attached to corporations.

One step further, the *Buckley v. Valeo* (1976) case allowed for a judicial interpretation that redefines freedom of speech to include the use of monetary assets as speech itself. This decision coupled with the most recent case, *Citizens United v. the Federal Election Commission*, gives corporations the ability to use their monetary assets as a form of free speech. The court decided again, and in no way implied, that corporations are people too. Unlike in the South Pacific Railroad Company, where the court believed that taxing them placed an undue burden that was unfair and not equally applied, the Citizens United case went a bit further. They argued that limiting the amount of money (the new definition of freedom of speech) was limiting the corporation's access to full participation in the political process. These decisions altered the role of corporations and the power of the government to fully implement sound regulation in the best interest of all citizens. Arguably, these decisions also have progressively changed the power within the government to justly hold corporations accountable as individuals.

A BRIEF HISTORY OF ECONOMIC REGULATION

© Jub-Job/Shutterstock.com

Economic regulation became more of an apparent need in the United States after the Great Depression. On October 29th, 1929, the United States saw economic devastation that changed how our government responds to financial crisis. If the Great Depression (1929–1930) didn't happen then our government may not have been culturally prepared to act as swiftly as they did during the bank bailouts (2008–2009).

During and after The Great Depression, farmers lost everything, which caused food shortages. Banks and businesses closed with 24 hours or less notice. People were forced to leave town to hide from creditors. The economy had plummeted and the idea of a free market unregulated by the government was no longer a luxury that corporations and bank had.

By the end of 1929, the economy declined by 40%, and this created a domestic and international financial crisis for over a decade. A variety of steps were taken by presidential leadership to engage all branches of the government in, not only regulating, but preventing this problem from happening in the future through government spending and threats of structural intervention.

Franklin D. Roosevelt defined the highest esteem of a democratic president. One that works through a crisis by creating social and economic programs to strengthen the economy, rebuild or create new infrastructure, and develop opportunities for citizens to care for their families. These are three things among the many that FDR was able to accomplish during his administration, which led to an unprecedented three terms as president.

REAGANOMICS—REAGAN'S RISE TO POWER

Famous for backing the trickle-down theory, championing elite conservative issues, and over using the term "welfare queen," Ronald Reagan has been the example of what good Republican values are since he was elected President in 1981. He'd been gaining momentum in politics for the previous decade, running against President Gerald Ford for the presidency in 1976, and then giving support to him once Ford gained the upper-hand during the campaign. However, once he became president in 1981, there was no denying the political power that he had accrued since deciding to take a turn into politics from being a famous Hollywood actor, effectively showcasing how it is possible to win an election based solely on star power, good communication skills, and promising to make it easier for rich people to keep their money.

Throughout history, these have been unspoken tenets to any election. Though many people would point out these qualities in previous elections and campaigns as criticism or satirical comedy, there was still a measure of legitimacy to the previous candidates, at least because they had years of previous experience from a career in politics. President Reagan marked one of the first celebrities-turned-political figures in a new trend of popular people lending their expertise to politics, essentially taking advantage of people's affection for him as an actor rather than his political resume, experience, or ideologies as they relate to citizens.

It was during his presidency in the 1980s that the concept of trickle-down theory became a well-publicized economic strategy. Dubbed "Reaganomics," the trickle-down theory allows the elite to receive tax cuts with the assumption that it would serve as economic stimulus and "trickle down" to those in the working class through job creation and more economic growth.

The ultimate result of Reaganomics was not that the rich created new jobs. The tax cuts meant that they were able to hold onto their money and wield more power in the political realm. Since then, though there have been modest tax increases across the board for all citizens, there is still a major disparity between the taxes lower- and middle-class citizens have to pay and what the upper-middle and upper class pay.

Furthermore, Reagan's economic legacy has contributed to the widening income disparity between the working class and the wealthy that has been steadily growing since Reaganomics went into effect. The trickle-down theory has been in wide use since then in many ways, including the reluctance that Congress has shown in raising the elite's taxes.

President Reagan also went down in infamy for labeling black women, and other women of color, "welfare queens." Many people saw this as classist and racist as poverty was problematized and personalized. Reagan was key in drilling down the idea of the bootstrap mentality within a person's individual life.

We live in a country that has created policies that go against those who are increasingly being pushed out of urban centers due to gentrification. Leaving many families without access to transportation, work, and viable education or vocational options for self-improvement. In the United States we readily cut taxes for the wealthy while inflating the cost of goods (for the average person) and while also being more than reluctant to raise the minimum wage.

This, in addition to Nancy Reagan's campaign titled the "War on Drugs," is responsible for the rising prison population in the last 30 years. The economic deregulation and the expansion of private sector corporations influencing the government, makes a compelling case that the Reagan administration was primarily built around protecting elite white men and their interests.

SOCIAL INEQUALITIES IN TABLES

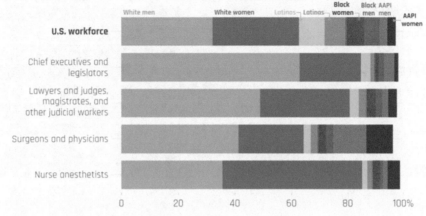

Black and Latinx workers are underrepresented in highest-paying occupations
Gender and racial/ethnic compositions of highest-paying U.S. occupations, 2015-2018

Source: Author's calculations using American Community Survey data, 2014–2018 5-year estimates.

Most Respondents Think Their Workplace is Above Average for Gender Equality

Percent of each group that said there was equal opportunity for men and women in most workplaces or their own workplace

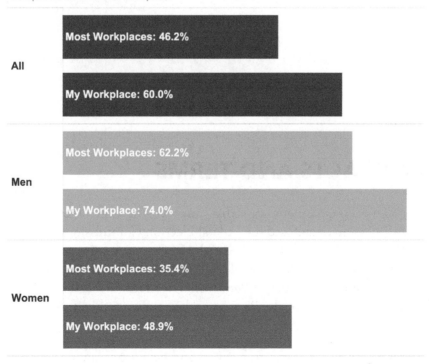

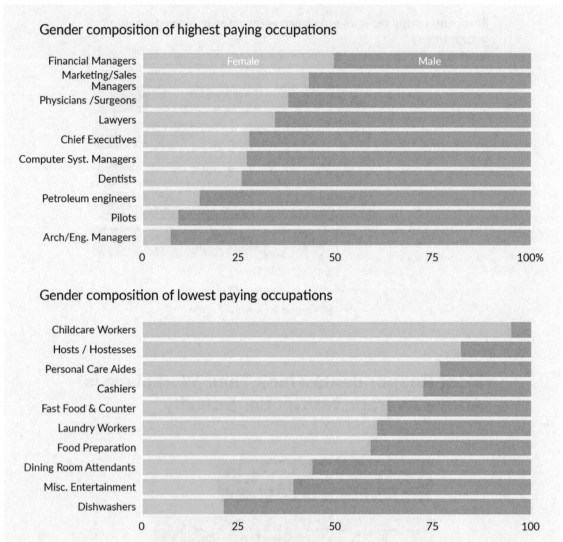

The enduring U.S. divide between men and women at work
The gender composition of the highest- and the lowest-paying U.S. occupations, 2015

Gender composition of highest paying occupations

Gender composition of lowest paying occupations

Source: Author's compilation of available gender composition data for broad occupational categories with highest and lowest mean wages according to Bureau of Labor Statistics tables "May 2015 National Occupational Employment and Wage Estimates" and "Employed persons by detailed occupation, sex, race, and Hispanic or Latino ethnicity."

Equitable Growth

IMPORTANT FACTS AND TERMS

Buckley v. Valeo: A 1976 Supreme Court case that amended the Federal Election Campaign Act of 1971, as amended in 1974 and established the Federal Election Commission (FEC), that were deemed unconstitutional. The Supreme Court upheld that the FEC was constitutionally within its rights to limit the contributions any one candidate could receive in an election, disclose the provisions and records of the FECA, and public financing of Presidential elections. The case decided that limiting how much a candidate could spend, except the President who receives public funding, and how the FEC appoints members was unconstitutional.

Civil code: The statutes and laws that govern business and negligence lawsuits and practices.

Corporate personhood: The concept that a corporation can be recognized as an individual in the eyes of the law. This grants the corporation the same rights as an individual, often allowing the executives of the corporation to take advantage of various loopholes and further taking advantage of its employees and those who are affected by the corporation's decisions.

Full faith and credit clause: A phrase in Article IV, Section 1 of the Constitution which dictates that a larger American government entity can help to alleviate the debts of a smaller, less stable government entity of the United States. This particular act is reminiscent of the bank bailout that recently took place, considering many banks are unofficially considered governmental entities.

International Monetary Fund (IMF): Founded in 1944 and inspired by the Great Depression's effect on international economies, the International Monetary Fund (IMF) is in charge of monitoring and regulating international monetary transactions, which includes determining the exchange rate.

Labor exploitation: Taking advantage of people through forcing labor out of them for personal and economic gain.

North American Free Trade Agreement (NAFTA): The North American Free Trade Agreement (NAFTA) was signed into law in 1993 by former President Clinton went into effect on January 1, 1994 and essentially eradicated any tariffs on goods traded between the United States, Canada, and Mexico. NAFTA critics worried that American jobs would inevitably start funneling to Mexico, exposing Americans to unemployment and exploiting Mexican workers.

Open Door Policy: Notes written by former Secretary of State John Hay in 1899 to China, which encouraged China to allow different nations to trade with them without any regulations or tariffs, essentially keeping the door open for economic trade opportunities. Although China was unsure of this agreement because there was no apparent economic benefit, they accepted so as not to insult the United States.

Organization of Petroleum Exporting Countries (OPEC): An organization founded in 1960 to support the world leaders in oil exporting. Essentially a who's who of all of the wealthiest nations. OPEC as a whole has a large influence on the overall economic outlook.

Santa Clara County v. Southern Pacific Railroad: An 1886 Supreme Court case wherein the Southern Pacific Railroad refused to pay taxes to Santa Clara County on the grounds that the Southern Pacific started in Missouri, so California has no rights to tax it. This case helped set the precedent for corporate personhood.

World Bank: Started in 1947 as party of the Marshall Plan to help rebuild Europe after World War II, the World Bank has been funding various government projects since then.

Link: https://usafacts.org/state-of-the-union/standard-living/

The wealth of the middle 20% of income earners has grown 66% since 1990.

REFERENCES

Katznelson, I., Kessleman, M., & Draper, A. (2009) The Politics of Power: A Critical Introduction to American Government.

CHAPTER SIX

Resistance Against Community and State Violence

© Luigi Morris/Shutterstock.com

This history of violence in the United States its first story to be told. While some hold a narrative of innocent people fleeing from Europe to free themselves from religious persecution that it not the full story. They were complicit and benefited from enslaved people in order to support their mission across the Atlantic. They used the forced labor of black people to build the American economy. This bondage was violence and that's the beginning of the story of the U.S.

Any positive political change movement in the United States should also be a movement for nonviolence. All suppression and oppression is violent, therefore the alleviation of such harm is about nonviolence and the prevention of harm. Learning about the impact of social and impact forces, requires you to also learn about how violence has played a role in our society and what can be done about it.

When trying to understand what violence has looked like over the years, we must look at the history of the communities used by the system. In Chapters 1 and 2 you learned about the ways in which our historical debts to indigenous people and other communities of color play a major role in what we see happening in our society today. The fight for Black Lives Matter, the rallying of support to stop Asian Pacific Islander hate crimes, and the battles around immigration and citizenship are everyday conversations in our nation.

What does history tell us? A prime example of legalized violence and denial of personhood is The Negro Act of 1740. This was a foundation piece of what was later used to craft slave codes. The act essentially deemed those who were enslaved as "property" and that they should be kept in "due subjection and obedience". The passage and implementation of this act made self-defense, literacy, and access to firearms illegal. This of course came almost 100 years before the Dred Scott v. Sandford decision that solidified that people of African descent, regardless if they were free or enslaved, had no rights of privileges that the U.S. constitution conferred to American citizens. This act of removal of personhood and the removal of protections and rights are what we called state sanctioned violence. "Similarly, the right to self-defense was quashed in the seventeenth-century Virginia, denied in Cincinnati in 1841, machine gunned into oblivion in 1919 Elaine, Arkansas, and brutally denied to Trayvon Martin, Kathryn Johnston, and Breonna Taylor" (Anderson, 2021, pg. 161).

Community violence is directly connected to the violence that the state perpetuates against it's "own" people. The violence from the state is rooted in maintaining the status quo. Protection of private property is generally prioritized over protecting people. This was seen in Oakland, California, during the protests demanding justice for the murder of Oscar Grant. Veterans, mothers, teenagers were peacefully assembling. The police beat people and arrested them. Many news agencies reported that vandalism was a cause for harsh police reactions rather than focusing on the hundreds, if not thousands, of lives taken by the Oakland Police Department. This double standard does not make for a strong democracy, and it does not provide us with safety. The kind of safety that allows for us to heal and grow.

There are various dialogues on institutional violence perpetrated either through bending laws that were initially put in place to protect American citizens or completely ignoring them all together. Change is impossible if people are fearful that, by putting action behind their words, they will be putting themselves in danger for demanding what is supposedly a human right. Fear is the greatest tool utilized by the state to reduce the amount of resistance you show to the injustices you face. Rather than waiting for you to become wiser about the levels of subjugation, they have dumbed down our education system so you don't even think you have a chance.

The rights to freedom of speech and the press has been a thorn in the government's side since they were originally written into the Constitution. It is as if the ruling classes thought the Founding Fathers wrote these laws in theory only. In 2016 that theory is still not fully practiced.

Despite what the American discourse has been, there is little way to deny that, if the white supremacist power structure continues, there will be egregious abuses of power, abuse which commonly has historical links to human exploitation and suffering. The body is a sacred vessel. All people have inalienable rights of self-determination to honor, preserve, and protect their own bodies. When even these simple rights have no real value and can be completely battered in a country that prides itself on being fair to all people, there is something fundamentally wrong with the system.

The real danger of American government-sanctioned violence against its own citizens is that it is not limited to bodily harm. While this is the most obvious, there are methods by which people can be tortured that do not leave bruises and lacerations and, therefore, do not heal nearly as easily. There are the various ways that the government is allowed to use surveillance and intimidation to scare people into silence; more recently, a favorite has been to use the threat of deportation and imprisonment for small infractions to keep people quiet. While American media is busy criticizing Russia's oppressive tactics and how overtly they censor their citizens, American methods can be significantly more dangerous because people are unaware of them. Or if there is awareness, they have been downgraded to conspiracy theories. The idea that the NSA has the ability to casually monitor a citizen's daily activities does not seem problematic, until an innocent person is arrested for contacting someone who happens to know someone who knows someone suspected of terrorism. The American love affair with "national security" has made it possible to enforce bigotry and xenophobia through abuse of power, distorting laws for personal and political gain, and covert intimidation.

However, there has also been a history of political resistance being a strong catalyst for change. Throughout history, the brave few who were willing to put themselves in danger for the greater good have been able to make change possible. One example would be how the Civil Rights movement was fought through mostly nonviolent political resistance with sit-ins, protests, marches, and student organizing. More recently, in 2009, the local uprising that took place when Oscar Grant was shot and killed by BART police officer, Johannes Mehserle, demonstrated how to maintain a nonviolent and strong voice in the face of incompetence. Although the demands from the Occupy movement were unclear because they were so numerous and so the movement was shorter lived than hoped for, what it lacked in duration, it made up for in strength and resonance.

The ultimate goal was to expose the 1% by putting a spotlight on how Wall Street both caused and benefited from the devastating 2008 recession, as well as previous corporate and government abuses of power. The key to any successful political resistance is making sure that those in power become aware that the people are paying attention by demanding that changes be made to the flawed system. No matter how long, short, loud, or quiet a movement is, it is the people's responsibility to hold the government and corporations accountable for the exploitation that affects them. If the people don't do it, no one else will.

This chapter explores various methodologies and philosophies behind political resistance, what causes a movement to arise and gain traction, and how starting in the community to change local government is beneficial in changing national problems.

CONDITIONS THAT INSPIRE RESISTANCE

© a katz/Shutterstock.com

The United States of America is admittedly capitalistic and arguably democratic. With the passage of *Citizens United v. Federal Elections Commission*, the people of the United States had their votes trumped by corporate power. Advocacy groups, like the NRA, have spent millions of dollars to prevent gun restrictions (Stone, 2010). Some argue this contributes to the high levels of gun violence in this country. Citizens United allowed corporations like the NRA to use their funds through PACs to purchase TV, radio, and newspaper ads (Stone, 2010) to legitimize their claims of corporate personhood. With this reality in mind, our economic and political systems require a critical examination of capitalism and its role in violence.

Leiman (2010) states:

"Capitalism simultaneously represents a set of class relations and institutional needs, either continually shaped or influenced by class struggle. To a significant extent these needs condition the form that the class struggle takes at any given moment." (p. 175)

These sets of associations allow corporations, such as those who profit from gun advocacy, to actively participate in the political process with more political power than the individual. This is the American machine of capitalism. The machine metaphor points to the systemic and coordinated nature of the U.S. system that creates inequality and perpetuates violence. It is widely accepted that the slavery system built the early economic success of this nation and allowed for the country to rise as an economic power prior to the 20th Century (Zinn, 2003).

Boyd (1998) writes:

"At no point during the Atlantic slave trade was there an absence of resistance, despite the millions of African captives who succumbed to the relentless European firepower and brutality and found themselves packed in the hold of slave ships bound for the Americas." (p. 43)

From the Underground Railroad to slave revolts to the abolition of slavery, African Americans have resisted the status quo of institutional and social oppression. African American women in the United States developed a culture of resistance through centuries of brutalization and humiliation in the private and public spheres of society (Ross, 1992). "The ability of slaves to construct a viable subculture of their own (based on family, community and religion) undoubtedly enabled them to withstand some of the psychological debilitation caused by the harsh conditions of American slavery" (Leiman, 2010, p. 20). Light (2009) wrote, "within the antebellum South the ultimate form of resistance in the quest for recognition was the acknowledgement that one was not property, both rhetorically and through escape" (p. 2). Furthermore, the law does not function as a social mediator of relations between all people; instead, it is a tool that merely functions to protect the more privileged. For women, this refers to those who meet the requirements of hegemonic femininity, that is, white, middle-class, heterosexual, and able bodied (p. 138).

The long-standing relationship between violence within and directed at the black community is reflected in the ongoing debate (Davis, 1998; Lyon, 2010; Schlosser, 1998) on the oppressive structure of the U.S. prison–industrial complex in which more than half of all prisoners are people of color (Figure 3). "Almost ten percent of our population is locked up, and the percentage is worse among young Black men" (Lyon, 2010, para 2). Advocates see abolishment of the prison system and reform as potential strategies to resist institutional punishment (Davis, 2001).

ADDRESSING COMMUNITY AND STATE VIOLENCE

State violence is the abuse of power by the government that ignores or deliberately acts in ways that prevent the ability of individuals and groups to thrive. The figure below shows the disproportionate rate of incarceration for Latino, White, and Black males in the United States in comparison to their percentage of the population. The numbers are dismal. At first glance, you will notice that although Caucasian (white) people make up a sizable portion of the population, they do not make up the majority of those incarcerated. People of color, men and women, are the highest incarcerated groups in this country.

Conant (2010) quotes Santos de La Carillo, a delegate to Mexico's National Indigenous Congress, who asked:

"What does resistance mean? Resistance means to defend what belongs to us as indigenous people: territory, resources, culture. If among our peoples, we didn't have resistance, we would no longer exist as peoples. Thanks to our resistance, we have maintained our cultures." (p. 36)

Resisting violence does not only mean resisting violent individuals and shunning them from society; but it also means resisting the oppressive structures that have created the conditions for urban destruction. Rosa Parks did this when she asked the NAACP in Alabama to find legal support for Recy Taylor, who was brutally raped by a white mob in the mid-1940s (McGuire, 2010; Spratling, 2010). Tharps (2001) asserts that "African Americans have been staging various forms of resistance since pre-revolutionary days, and at the center of these movements is the struggle for existence and for cultural power" (p. 129).

Because personal experiences are innately political (Mills, 1959), when a person gains a sense of agency and ability to change their situation, I believe that regardless of the type of violation they experience, they are nonetheless resisting oppression and state violence.

White (2005) states that, "of course, Black women enter and depart the anti-violence movement at different historical moments" (p. 12). Many African American women demonstrated creative means of political resistance to lynching through education and the written word, such as Ida B. Wells (1862–1931).

Wells wrote for many years about the need to end slavery in order to bring about a larger sense of equity for all human beings. During the same time period, African American Josephine St. Pierre Ruffin (1842–1924) used her voice to influence women's leadership. "Ruffin and others in the public arena demonstrated keenly developed notions of self and a firm belief in the unprecedented role of Black women at the end of the nineteenth and the beginning of the twentieth century" (Hohl, 2010, p. x).

A BRIEF HISTORY OF BLACK RESISTANCE IN OAKLAND

The role of political resistance is deeply rooted in Oakland's past and present. This section presents a synopsis of Oakland political resistance to community and state violence from 1960, focusing mainly on the Black Panther Party and the effects of the crack epidemic, and examples of community action and transformation that is leading today.

Resistance in the Black community has come through a number of channels: communities of faith, various forms of creative expression (music, dance, performing arts, and theater), political activism, care-giving in the community, and methods of escape from oppressive institutions (Davis, 2001; Leiman, 2010; Light, 2009).

The Black Panther Party for Self Defense (BPP) was founded in Oakland in the late 1960s with its primary goal to sustain and protect the Black community. J. Edgar Hoover, first director of the Federal Bureau of Investigation (FBI), named the group "the greatest single threat" (Lee & Smith, 2002) to the internal security of the United States. Over-policing in communities of color became a common practice in Oakland (and other urban cities across the country) after the economic rise of African Americans during the changing post-World War II job market, from which women and people of color benefited (Nosotro, 2004).

In the late 1960s and 1970s, we saw the Black Panther Party (BPP) act as guardians and caregivers in the community. Their mission was to promote self-determination and demand safety from state violence and state interference in community life (Ginwright, 2010).

The group was discredited as "radical" and "left-wing," when in reality they were feeding children before and after school, walking people to and from work to, ironically, protect them from the police, and demanding equal protection under the law.

In the middle of the 20th century, one sign of state sponsored intervention presented itself in the 1954 Supreme Court case *Brown v. Board of Education*. The integration of schools was one of the loudest forms of state intervention against racism and bigotry within public institutions. Still, state interventions alone were not effective in creating long lasting change for "although the Brown decision was a great victory, its aftermath makes clear how insufficient an agreement between elites can be in changing a social order" (Higham, 1997, p. 4).

The BPP empathized with this perspective and took community change as a human right and a righteous responsibility. The Party took survival into their own hands. The aims and beliefs put forth by the Black Panther Party in 1967 (Figure 4) are one example of the strength and partnership within Oakland's Black community. The organization's work was in direct resistance to social and political conditions for African Americans across the country, to alleviate the impact of racism and classism on every aspect of Black life in the United States (Seale, 1974).

There were many aspects of the Black Panther Party that augmented the quality of life for the Oakland community. One of the most notable efforts was the Free Breakfast Program for children before school. This form of organizing and resistance is the type of cultural care necessary when the state will not distribute resources to all citizens equally. Although there were efforts to eliminate the oppression of black people based on race and class, the role of women in the Party was contentious at times

Brown (1996) considers black women to be essential to the success of local community programs. Along this vein, Matthews (1998) argues that women experienced violence within the Party, and that gendered and sexualized politics played a role in the development of the political party.

In the 1970s, the Black Panthers saw their activities disrupted because of the Counterintelligence Program (COINTELPRO), a program by the Federal Bureau of Investigation (FBI) that worked closely with the Oakland Police to discredit the BPP because of their revolutionary ideas and implementation of their 10-Point Plan.

By 1972, FBI operatives had infiltrated the organization, creating an atmosphere of mistrust amongst members and breaking down the foundational relationships and connections that had contributed to the organization's strength and success. By this time, a majority of the organization's leaders had been imprisoned or killed (Wolf, 1976). Between 1970 and 1980, the Black Panther Party saw its activities come to an end, with blue-collar jobs leaving Oakland, and an influx and spread of crack cocaine (Lang, 2000).

By 1980, the crack epidemic had taken hold in Oakland's civic and social life, mostly in East and West Oakland. Because crack was easy to produce, most drug dealers prepared the drug in their own residences. From the arrival of crack until 2000, Oakland remained in the top 10 cities hardest hit by the drug epidemic (Johnson, 2011). Due to unequally distributed "mandatory sentences" many black men and women were incarcerated due to unfair drug laws (Alexander, 2010).

Payton (2010) writes:

"Between 1981 and 1986, Oakland lost 2,051 private-sector jobs. In Alameda County, where Oakland is located, more than 14,000 jobs were lost between 1980 and 1983. The trend was happening all over the country, fueled by mergers, leveraged buyouts, and national tax policies that provided incentives for corporations to move overseas." (para. 4)

The crack epidemic, unemployment, and the destruction of the radical infrastructure created by the Black Panther Party not only removed tangible and physical benefits, but also killed hope and the political identity of Oakland communities (Ogbar, 2004). Sharpe (2005) writes about the impact that the crack epidemic had on black women. Although her work focused on poor black women in Atlanta, the social parallels offer relevance to this study. Some of the consequences of crack cocaine use among black women in Atlanta included sex-for-crack pregnancies; crack induced paranoia, and constant desperation and urgency. Sharpe argues that the crack epidemic is reminiscent of Jim Crow, and she also "questions the social and political structures that created a climate that effectively shuts down access to viable life chances for poor black women" (West, 2007, p 181). In addition to destroying individual lives, the crack epidemic changed family relations, the political structure of Oakland, and the local economic development.

In the 1990s, Oakland suffered from a $34 million budget deficit, a rise in homicides and imprisonment among young black men, and a mass exodus of the employers who provided wealth for the city in terms of tax revenue. The budget deficit not only affected city politics but also economic conditions for people of color throughout the city. "By 1990, 18.5% of Oakland residents, many of them African American, were struggling under the federal poverty level, versus only 10% poverty in neighboring communities in Alameda County" (Clark & Lin, 2009, p. 19).

In the early 2000s, Oakland saw a further rise in violence. Rand (2007) reported that, "in response to rising crime and violence in the early 2000s, Oakland, California, voters passed the Violence Prevention and Public Safety Act of 2004" (para 1). These funds are used to help alleviate some of the social consequences to violence through a multi-pronged approach. The nearly $19 million is used for

Fire Services, Police Officers and Youth Violence Prevention program. This program is also known as Measure Y (described above).

The Alameda County Domestic Violence Report (2003) stated that "there were a total of 122 deaths related to domestic violence in Alameda County from 1996 to 2000, an average of 24 deaths each year. A child was present in over half the incidents (55%) that included reports of who was at the scene" (p. 9). Additionally it was reported that "one of Oakland's greatest challenges is the crisis of street violence gripping it and many of America's under-invested inner cities, exacting a high toll on residents and communities" (Clark & Lin, 2009, p. 1). Spiker et al. (2009) reported that within one year, from 2006 to 2007, African Americans totaled nearly 70% of all homicides in the city of Oakland. "In 2008, Oakland lost 125 people from the community to murder, down by 1.6 percent from the 2007 total of 127" (p. 2).

Violence creates a culture of isolation among youth and adults; experiences of violation break down community ties and destroy chances toward commonalities being recognized. The violence also lends itself to PTSD among youth of color in Oakland, affecting their academic achievement, and creating a cycle wherein they must join, and become victim to the violence in order to survive. Collectively, Oakland residents experience all social problems together. West Oakland has historically been a black neighborhood (Pearlman, 2012). West Oakland "once had the largest population in the city" (Ginwright, 2010, p. 27).

This region has seen a lot of economic violence that has negatively impacted people's lives in that region, and the city at large. In economically strapped areas like West Oakland, city officials worked with developers to create new housing and to bring new business to Oakland. The only catch was that those who were currently living in West Oakland would not be able to afford the rent or mortgage in these new housing structures which ended up displacing low-income black residents. "From 1997 to 2004 the average sale price of homes in West Oakland rose from $53,317 to $315,000. Nearly 80% of West Oakland residents are renters. More than 2/3 of renters are very low or low income" (Letz, 2007, para. 10). This form of economic violence provides an example of living in the nuances of unequal protection under the law. The social factors that promote the literal and figurative displacement of African Americans and other people of color in Oakland have created a system in which the conditions that a person lives in can be the strongest factor in the perpetuation of violence. This is one of the reasons why advocates and residents are concerned about gentrification and environmental degradation as social and state levels of violence being perpetrated against low-income communities. In 2007, Just Cause of Oakland [known today and Causa Justa: Just Cause] organized a Gentrification Tour in West Oakland where they took leaders, residents, and other interested community members around the neighborhood to see the impact of this economic strategy to remove blight from economically disadvantaged areas. One of the consequences of gentrification has been a decrease in the African American population citywide. Allen-Taylor (2011) reported: "Oakland's African American population plummeted from 142,000 (38 percent) in 2000 to 109,000 (28 percent) in 2010" (para. 2).

IDEA—Read in a circle of friends and family silently or have one person read it aloud. When you're done, take some time to digest what she says and discuss your reactions.

Lynching Law in America
Chicago, 1900
Founder: Memphis Free Press
Ida B Wells

Prevention and Enforcement in the Hate Crime Crisis

Contributed by Michael Guzy

Introduction

Since their origins in the civil rights movements of the 1960s, "bias crimes"—more commonly referred to as "hate crimes"—have become a key tool in the fight against the various forms of discriminatory violence that affect many identities. In a country as diverse as the United States, and one where that diversity is fraught with many underlying tensions and material inequities, the various hate crime statutes that dot this country are a realization of decades of civil rights organizing and activism. As with most criminal law, hate crime statutes have a preventative rationale—they discourage hate crime from occurring—as well as mechanisms that encourage the enforcement of such law. Hate crime law, however, seems to be failing in achieving effective prevention *and* enforcement; hate crimes both seem to be continually increasing (Balsamo, 2020), and massive gaps in enforcement leave many hate crimes unanswered for and unreported (Li, 2019). This article will give an overview of the mechanics, intentions, and overall history of hate crime law, and will attempt to glean from it the various tensions and issues that hate crime legislation is currently facing. Ultimately, this article will find that both the preventative and enforcement framework holding together hate crime laws is both flawed and incomplete, and efforts to reduce hate crimes should also consider non-legal solutions in order to effectively counter hatred in the country once and for all.

A Brief Primer on Hate Crimes

Succinctly, hate crimes are crimes directed at a victim *because* of a certain characteristic they have or appear to have. The most common characteristics listed in the various statutes that exist presently include race, ethnicity, religion, gender, sex, and disability. In practice, this formulation leaves convicting someone on a hate crime charge a challenge, as one must prove that the crime was inspired by a hatred of an individual's characteristic. Being convicted of a hate crime typically means that one receives an "enhanced" sentence on top of an already existing sentence. Many states also have separate hate crime statutes that target more specific crimes individually, defacing a place of worship, for example, is sometimes a charge all on its own. This kind of sentencing structure, though seemingly unique, is less novel than it seems, it is the same mode of thinking that differentiates a third-degree murder charge with a first-degree murder charge, intent matters in crime, and hate crime often is just an added indicator of intent (Shively, 2005).

Sentence enhancement is also justified legally through the unique harms hate crimes present. A single hate crime has a ripple effect which impacts far more than an individual and their close ones, it impacts whole communities. Hate crimes suggest to groups that they are *not welcome* into the social fold, and thus instill them with fear and confusion, which has an impact that extends far beyond their immediate communities (Bell & Perry, 2015; McDevitt, Balboni, Garcia, & Gu, 2001; Noelle, 2002).

Hate Crime, Hate Speech, and Prevention

In spite of the very real harms that hate crime fosters, the topic of *hate speech*, often associated with hate crimes, runs into contact with constitutional protections under the first amendment. The Supreme Court has consistently upheld hate speech as a legal activity as long as it passes an "imminent danger" test, wherein the speech is neither "directed at inciting or producing imminent lawless action" and "likely to produce or incite such action" (Supreme Court of the United States, 1968, p. 447). Which are both high bars to pass.

This presents a dilemma for prevention, as hate speech can lead to and inspire hate crimes without a legible link of "imminent danger." Hate speech can foster communities that utilize hate crimes as tactics, and it can be used to spread fear in much the same ways that hate crimes can, often in inconspicuous ways (Gottschalk, 2018). On the other hand, however, crossing the line into free speech in regard to hate speech can further entrench state crackdowns upon other forms of speech, as *many* forms of speech can be read as implicitly doing the same things that hate speech does.

The "preventative" task of hate crime legislation is thus often unable to get to what is often the core of what causes hate crime, and efforts to get at that core pose a risk to certain democratic freedoms. The solution, as such, should be two-fold, for one, we should increase our efforts of calling out hate speech whenever it is present, drown out such speech from public spaces and report such speech in private spaces, make it difficult for the toxic ideas presented in that speech from infesting and motivating others. Secondly, we must educate and inform as many people as possible of the common characteristics of hate speech and the common ways it can spread, and reform and teach those convicted of hate crimes of techniques and strategies that may reduce their hatred.

A Brief History of Hate (And Its Discontents)

The United States has a sordid history with hate, and it has provoked it through both state and non-state means. Slavery, the brutal massacres and genocides of Indigenous people, the illegalization of homosexuality and queerness in general, were advanced through a tandem acceptance between the government and the public that it was *right* to hate and discriminate against an "other." The Civil Rights Acts of the 1960's changed this model but did not fully confront the depth of bitter hatred that the state itself helped to invoke for centuries. The steady stream of federal hate crime laws since, such as Title I of 1968 Civil Rights Act, the Violent Crime Control and Law Enforcement Act of 1994, and The Matthew Shepard and James Byrd Jr. Hate Crimes Prevention Act, alleviate, but fail to fully confront, hate crime.

These laws, only meant towards *federal* crimes, left the great majority of hate crime-oriented work to the states. The effort to create state statutes against hate crimes began in the early 1980's, with Washington and Oregon putting the first resolutions in place in 1981 (Shively, 2005). States have steadily introduced and reformed hate crime statutes ever since. Work has been continual in implementing new characteristics that would be protected under hate crime laws, with gender and sexuality often being recent characteristics added onto hate crime statutes. Furthermore, coordination between federal and state governments, driven by the Hate Crime Statistics Act of 1990, have sharpened data collection efforts regarding hate crimes considerably.

Hatred and Enforcement

However, the unequal distribution of hate crime measures and identities covered under hate crime law have led to an uneven patchwork of enforcement regarding hate crimes. Ohio, for instance, has no statute covering discrimination against sexuality, while the states of Arkansas, North Dakota, South Carolina, and Wyoming have no hate crime statute whatsoever, making data collection all the more difficult and enforcement essentially non-existent for non-federal related offenses. Even in states with generally complete hate crime statutes, different local situations vary enforcement and reporting immensely, and that often comes down to individuals trusting the authorities to hear their statements and respond accordingly—authorities which often have a very fraught historical *and* contemporary relationship with marginalized groups. Hate crime statutes, as such, can lead authorities awkwardly confronting a social situation they helped make with inadequate tools to enforce them.

Enforcement against hate crimes, then, not only is incomplete, but also fundamentally rests on problematic grounds, many groups have justifiable reasons why they do not want to report to the authorities about their strife, despite it perhaps being in their best interest. Efforts to "increase enforcement" will not change this fact. A change to this would require both a *political* response, and an *anti-political*—or non-profit based—response. A political response would require states and the federal government to adopt measures that would increase the equity of all, and measures that reduce the necessity of the police on all fronts. These are rather optimistic goals, which leaves the *anti-political* response a necessary one in the meantime. This would continue the profusion of non-profit organizations into the sphere of hate crime work, allowing them to address whatever trauma has occurred, and act as a liaison between the victim and the various systems and institutions they must navigate to get justice.

Conclusion

In conclusion, the emergence of hate crime laws, while an important and inspiring narrative in a country which has so much baggage when it comes to hatred and discrimination, should not be considered a panacea when it comes to dealing with discrimination in this country. The key difficulty of hate crime statutes is that they graft what is ultimately a *legal* solution onto what is essentially a larger *political* problem, and they will always be limited in that sense. This does not mean that hate crime statutes should be thrown-out, on the contrary, they hold an important place on the frontlines against hatred in this country when nothing else works; however, the continued proliferation and increase in hate crimes across the country show the natural limitations of such law, and our generally lackluster efforts in fighting hatred in other areas. If we are to decrease hatred in these times of intense polarization and political tension, we must begin by understanding and addressing hate in a more holistic way.

IMPORTANT FACTS AND TERMS

Brown v. Board of Education: A legendary Supreme Court case in 1954 that reversed the *Plessy v. Ferguson* (1896) that dictated the "separate but equal" rule. *Brown v. Board of Education* made it school integration legal and had other effects concerning the various segregation laws that were in place during the Civil Rights era.

Conscientious objector: A person who, for conscience or conscious reasons, refuses to enlist in the armed forces. A particularly popular practice as an act of protest during the Vietnam War when the draft was still being enforced.

Gentrification: The process of "improving" a neighborhood or region that has been run-down by waiting until the property value is low and then buying the property, then pushing out the residents and businesses that were there.

Marginalization: Forcefully relegating a group of people based on color, race, sex/gender, or belief to a powerless position in a society; oppression.

Police brutality: A common practice of severe abuse of police power which manifests itself in police harassment and excessive force during routine stops and arrests.

Sedition: Inciting a riot or political upheaval through speeches, protests, or conduct. Often punishable by law in many countries, including the United States.

Chapter 6

CRIME & JUSTICE

Over 6.4 million Americans were in prison, jail, or under probation or parole when counted in 2018, though an estimated 10.7 million people were admitted to jail throughout the year.

Nearly 90% of prisoners were in state prisons. The total number of prisoners in 2019 was down 11% from the 2009 peak due to shrinking state and federal prison populations.

https://usafacts.org/state-of-the-union/crime/

REFERENCES

Alameda County Domestic Violence Collaborative. (2003). *A profile of family violence in Alameda County: A call for action.* Prepared by Maternal Child and Adolescent Health Section, Community Assessment Planning and Education Unit in the Alameda County Public Health Department. Retrieved from http://www.acphd.org/data-reports/reports-by-topic/domestic-violence.aspx

Alexander, M. (2010). The New Jim Crow: Mass Incarceration in the Age of Colorblindness. New York: The New Press.

Allen-Taylor, J. (2011). Bring back the Black. *Race, Poverty and the Environment, 18*(1). http://urbanhabitat.org/18-1/allen-taylor (Retrieved December 1, 2012)

Anderson, C. (2021) The Second. Race and Guns in a Fatally Unequal America. Bloomsbury: New York.

Balsamo, M. (2020, November 16). Hate crimes in US reach highest level in more than a decade. *AP News.* Retrieved from https://apnews.com/article/hate-crimes-rise-FBI-data-ebbcadca8458aba96575da905650120d

Bell, J.G., & Perry, B. (2015). Outside looking in: The community impacts of anti-lesbian, gay, and bisexual hate crime. *Journal of Homosexuality, 62*(1), 98–120. doi:10.1080/00918369.2014.957133

Boyd, H. (1998). Radicalism and resistance: The evolution of Black radical thought. *The Black Scholar, 28*(1), 43.

Brown, A. (1996. Women and the Black Panther Party: An Interview with Angela Brown. *Socialist Review. 26*(1-2), 33–67.

Conant, J. (2010). A Poetics of Resistance: The revolutionary public relations of the Zapatista Insurgency. AK Press: Oakland.

Davis, A. (1998). Masked Racism: Reflections on the Prison Industrial Complex. http://www.thirdworldtraveler.com/Prison_System/Masked_Racism_ADavis.html (Retrieved January 20, 2011)

Davis, A. (2001). Public Imprisonment and Private Violence: Reflections on the Hidden Punishment of Women. In Marguerite R. Waller & Jennifer Rycenga (Eds.), *Women, War & Resistance: Frontline Feminisms.* New York: Routledge.

Ginwright. S. (2010). Black Youth Rising: Activism and Radical Healing in Urban America. New York: Teachers College Press.

Gottschalk, S. (2018). Accelerators, amplifiers, and conductors: A model of tertiary deviance in online white supremacist networks. *Deviant Behavior, 41*(7), 841–855. doi:10.1080/01639625.2020.1734746

Healy, J. (2010). Oscar Grant or Lebron James? The Systemic Devaluation of Black Life in America. *Tikkun. 25*(6), 25–26.

Higham, J. (1997). Civil Rights and Social Wrongs: Black – White Relations Since World War II. University Park, PA: Pennsylvania State Press.

Hohl, E (2010). The uplift ourselves and our race: The New Negro woman of the 1890s. (Doctoral dissertation) Retrieved from ProQuest Dissertations and Theses database. (UMI No. AAT 3421725)

Johnson, S. (2011). The return of "Freeway" Ricky Ross, the man behind a crack empire. http://www.insidebayarea.com/ci_17113312?source=most_emailed (Retrieved January 20, 2011)

Lang, C. (2000). The New Global and Urban Order: Legacies For the "Hip Hop Generation". *Race and Society. 3*(2), 111–142.

Leiman, M. (2010). The Political Economy of Racism. Haymarket Books: Chicago.

Letz, J. (2007). The West Oakland Gentrification Tour! *Poor Magazine.* http://poormagazine.org/node/1776. Retrieved August 1, 2012)

Li, W. (2019, November 26). *Why police struggle to report one of the fastest-growing hate crimes.* Retrieved from The Marshall Project website: https://www.themarshallproject.org/2019/11/26/why-police-struggle-to-report-one-of-the-fastest-growing-hate-crimes

Lyon, A. (2010, August 18). The Prison Industrial Complex. *The Huffington Post.* Retrieved from http://www.huffingtonpost.com/andrea-lyon/the-prison-industrial-com_b_686582.html

Matthews, T. (1998) No one ever asks what a man's place in the revolution is: Gender and sexual politics in the Black Panther Party, 1966-1971. (Doctoral dissertation) Retrieved from ProQuest Dissertations and Theses database. (UMI No. AAT 9825298)

McDevitt, J., Balboni, J., Garcia, L., & Gu, J. (2001). Consequences for victims: A comparison of bias- and bon-bias-motivated assaults. *American Behavioral Scientist, 45*(4), 697–713. doi:10.117 7%2F0002764201045004010

McGuire, D. (2010). At the Dark End of the Street: Black Women, Rape, and Resistance – A New History of the Civil Rights Movements from Rosa Parks to the Rise of Black Power. New York: Knopf.

Mills, C. (1959). The Sociological Imagination. Chapter One: The Promise. http://legacy.lclark.edu/ ~goldman/socimagination.html (Retrieved December 20, 2010)

Noelle, M. (2002). The ripple effect of the Matthew Shepard murder: Impact on the assumptive worlds of members of the targeted group. *American Behavioral Scientist, 46*(1), 27–50. doi:10.11 77%2F0002764202046001004

Ogbar, J. (2004). Black Power: Radical Politics and African American Identity. Baltimore, Maryland: Johns Hopkins University Press.

Payton, B. (2010). The Root Cities: Oakland's Economic Power. *The Root.* http://www.theroot.com/ views/root-cities-oakland-s-economic-power (Retrieved February 7, 2012)

Pearlman, L. (2012). The Sky's the Limit People V. Newton, the Real Trial of the 20th Century? Berkeley, CA: Regent Press.

Seale, B. (1974). Part 3 of Chapel Hill Speech: Bobby Seale: It's the Masses of People Who are Really Radical. *The Black Panther.* http://solomon.bltc.alexanderstreet.com/cgi-bin/asp/philo/bltc/get-doc.pl?S14105-D010 (Retrieved January 20, 2011)

Sharpe, T. (2005) Behind the Eight Ball: Sex for Crack Cocaine Exchange and Poor Black Women. New York: The Haworth Press: Binghamton.

Shively, M. (2005). *Study of literature and legislation on hate crime in America* [Web Document]. Retrieved from the National Institute of Justice website: https://www.ojp.gov/pdffiles1/nij/ grants/210300.pdf

Spiker, S., Garvey, J., Arnold, K., & Williams, J. (2009). Homicides in Oakland. 2008 homicide report: An analysis of homicides in Oakland from January through December 2008. http://www. urbanstrategies.org/programs/infotech/documents/2008_Homicide_Report.pdf

Stone, P. (2010). Anti-Terror Efforts Put NRA Under The Gun. *National Journal.* May 14.

Supreme Court of the United States. (1968). *U.S. reports: Brandenburg v. Ohio, 395 U.S. 444.* [Periodical]. Retrieved from the Library of Congress website: https://www.loc.gov/item/usrep395444/

Wolf, P. (1976, April 23). Supplementary detailed staff reports on intelligence activities and the rights of Americans. Retrieved from http://www.icdc.com/~paulwolf/cointelpro/churchfinalreportIIIa. htm (Retrieved November 1, 2010)

Zinn, H. (2003). A People's History of the United States. 1492 – present. HarperCollins: NY.

CHAPTER SEVEN

Human Rights, Civil Rights and The Movements For Equity

For the first time in American social and political discourse, systemic racism has become a part of our mainstream reality. We talk, learn, and organize around issues of police brutality, housing discrimination, gender inclusion, and immigrant rights - all issues that are exacerbated by inequality. Often times we are talk about inequity as something that just happens, that isn't necessarily done by people. This is not the case. Inequality in our social and political systems are deeply entrenched in policy (written by people) and enforced or ignored by people.

Civil liberties have been defined as the parameters of activities that are sanctioned under governmental protection. Our civil liberties are basic rights and protections an individual has the right to engage in without excessive interference from the government. These have included the freedom of religion, speech, press, petition, and assembly. Arguably, the ways in which these freedoms are protected varies by group.

The U.S. government considers civil liberties to be those protected by the Bill of Rights, and other amendments in the constitution. Civil Rights are legal protections. The cross over and confusion is met by judicial decisions that decide whether or not a particular act by the government is Constitutional. For example, *Trump v. Hawaii* deemed that his travel ban against Muslim countries as unconstitutional.

The Eighth Amendment states that citizens will not be subject to "cruel and unusual punishment." However, in some states, they still use death as punishment for violent crimes.

The interpretation of this varies by state. In Michigan, where they do not practice the death penalty, they do sentence people to life in prison.

In California, which is a death penalty state, Governor Gavin Newsom issued a maratorium in 2019 on the use of capital punishment. The death penalty is sanctioned violence by the state where death is used as a punishment for heinous or violent crimes. This is a controversial issue in the debate on civil liberties in this country.

CIVIL LIBERTIES & CIVIL RIGHTS

Civil liberties are personal guarantees and freedoms that the regime cannot abridge, either by law or by judicial interpretation. Though the scope of the term differs amongst sundry countries, some examples of civil liberties include the liberation from slavery and coerced labor, liberation from torture and death, the right to liberty and security, liberation of conscience, religion, expression, press, assembly and association, verbalization, the right to privacy, the right to equal treatment and due process, and the right to a fair tribulation, as well as the right to life. Other civil liberties include the right to own property, the right to forfend oneself, and the right to bodily integrity. Within the distinctions between civil liberties and other types of liberty, distinctions subsist between positive liberty/positive rights and negative liberty/negative rights.

IN UNDERSTANDING THE IMPACT OF STATE VIOLENCE

An individual's relationship to the state is based on the ability to participate and remain complicit to the status quo. Our society's status quo is based on an individual's access to resources and information. The status quo in the United States is structured on a white supremacist culture that favors individuals with white skin and those with high-income levels. A classist society is a society that can be easily controlled. This control comes from the political discourse that allows us to see oppression only in other countries, not in our own (Young, 1988); this makes people think they are not oppressed. A society of people who do not know they are oppressed is a problem in a democratic society that espouses liberty and justice. Justice, as defined by Young (1988):

Should not refer only to distribution, but also to the institutional conditions necessary for the development and exercise of individual capacities and collective communication and cooperation (p. 39).

Within this social structure we have a governing body that controls how we live our daily lives. The state acts as a conduit, not only for basic needs like water, food, and shelter, but also for power, safety, and order. When the state organizes itself through criminal means then the people are required to question authority and organize themselves to thrive without the rule of law.

State organized crime was considered by Chambliss (1989) who, in his presidential address to the American Society on Criminology, discussed his characteristics of state organized crime as an act that was committed by the state that is within their rule of law. This means that a government can make their once illegal activities legal. This was displayed in a complex manner during the murder of Oscar Grant and the trial of Bay Area Regional Transit (BART) police officer, Johannes Mehserle.

On January 1, 2009, Oscar Grant was shot and killed by white BART police officer, Johannes Mehserle. "Feeling the pressure, the Alameda County District Attorney charged Officer Mehserle with murder; Mehserle was the first cop hit with such a charge in California history" (Healy, 2010, p. 25). This case gained public support because the incident was digitally recorded from a witness's cell phone. Based on my understanding of state violence this was an act of terror.

However, due to the need for the criminal justice system to maintain the status quo of oppression in order to meet the needs of the prison industrial complex, the BART police officer who claimed he "accidentally" killed Oscar Grant got time served for the case and had the audacity to request his job back. Oscar's family lost their son, brother, nephew and grandson. Under the current definitions of state violence, these incidences of abuse of power in the police department go under-investigated and remain overlooked as a consequence of a bureaucratic system. If black lives mattered as much as white lives do in our society we wouldn't have these problems.

Violence and nonviolence is framed within a dominant political discourse of public safety (Alexander, 2010). This does a few things: Namely it eliminates the role of the state in perpetuating or causing dysfunction among people and groups.

Terming it "public safety" can easily lay the blame and responsibility on the people who suffer from structural injustice. This scapegoating allows for criminal justice policies that rely on stereotypes of black adults and youth (Alexander, 2010; Ginwright, 2001) and disengages the "public" from participating in their own path towards freedom.

From a humanistic perspective, the experiences of subjugated people do not define their character or value. Humanism "advocates [for] the extension of participatory democracy and the expansion of the open society, standing for human rights and social justice" (American Humanist Association, 2008, para 2).

The oppression of any people is a consequence of the governing structure and policies under which they live—how the system is structured provides the platform that we are all born into and that gives a person her lot in life. I first saw this connection in early 20th Century sociological works.

Mills (1959) wrote about the sociological imagination - arguing that our personal issues were connected to the larger structure of society. He wrote:

Yet people do not usually define the troubles they endure in terms of historical change and institutional contradiction. The well-being they enjoy, they do not usually impute to the big ups and downs of the societies in which they live. Seldom aware of the intricate connection between the patterns of their own lives and the course of world history… (para 3).

If this connection were applied to understanding of the state and its relationship to public life, I believe we could demand a change to the way leadership is practiced and find out how all people can participate in systemic change. Many believe that their personal troubles they experience are on the periphery to the real problems of the world. On the contrary, there is a deep connection to our personal problems as political problems. (Freccero, 1999).

https://github.com/washingtonpost/data-police-shootings

Hate Crimes

https://usafacts.org/data/topics/people-society/democracy-and-society/

INTRODUCTION

Since their origins in the civil rights movements of the 1960's, "bias crimes"—more commonly referred to as "hate crimes"—have become a key tool in the fight against the various forms of discriminatory violence that affect many identities. In a country as diverse as the United States, and one where that diversity is fraught with many underlying tensions and material inequities, the various hate crime statutes that dot this country are a realization of decades of civil rights organizing and activism. As with most criminal law, hate crime statutes have a preventative rationale—they discourage hate crime from occurring—as well as mechanisms that encourage the enforcement of such law. Hate crime law, however, seems to be failing in achieving effective prevention and enforcement; hate crimes both seem to be continually increasing, and there are still massive gaps in enforcement which leaves many hate crimes unanswered for and unreported. This article will give an overview of the mechanics, intentions, and overall history of hate crime law, and will attempt to glean from it the various tensions and issues that hate crime legislation is currently facing. Ultimately, this article will find that both the preventative and enforcement framework holding together hate crime laws is both flawed and incomplete, and efforts to reduce hate-crimes should also consider non-legal solutions in order to effectively counter hatred in the country once and for all.

A BRIEF PRIMER ON HATE CRIMES

Succinctly, hate crimes are crimes directed at a victim *because* of a certain characteristic they have or appear to have. The most common characteristics listed in the various statutes that exist presently include, race, ethnicity, religion, gender, sex, and disability. In practice, this leaves actually convicting someone on a hate crime charge a challenge, as one must prove that the crime was inspired by a hatred of an individual's characteristic. Being convicted of a hate crime typically means that one receives an "enhanced" sentence on top of an already existing sentence. Many states also have separate hate crime statutes that target more specific crimes individually, defacing a place of worship, for example, is sometimes charge all on its own. This kind of sentencing structure, though seemingly unique, is less novel than it seems, it is the same mode of thinking that differentiates a third-degree murder charge with a first-degree murder charge, intent matters in crime, and hate crime often is just an added indicator of intent.

Sentence enhancement is also justified legally through the unique harms hate crimes present. A single hate crime has a ripple effect which impacts far more than an individual and their close ones, it impacts whole communities, it suggests to groups that they are *not welcome* into the social fold, and thus instills them with fear and confusion which has very many impacts that extend far beyond their communities.

HATE CRIME, HATE SPEECH, AND PREVENTION

In spite of the very real harms that hate crime fosters, the topic of *hate speech*, often associated with hate crimes, runs into contact with constitutional protections under the first amendment. The Supreme Court has consistently upheld hate speech as a legal activity as long as it passes an "imminent danger" test, wherein the speech is neither "directed at inciting or producing imminent lawless action" and "likely to produce or incite such action" (*Brandenburg v. Ohio*, 1969). Which are both rather high bars to pass.

This presents a dilemma for prevention, as hate speech can lead to and inspire hate crimes without a legible link of "imminent danger." Hate speech can foster communities that utilize hate crimes as tactics, it can be used to spread fear in much the same ways that hate crimes can and is often provoked in stealthier ways than hate crimes can be, as it is often intangible and online. On the other hand, however, crossing the line into free speech in regard to hate speech can further entrench state crackdowns upon other forms of speech, as *many* forms of speech can be read as implicitly doing the same things that hate speech does.

The "preventative" task of hate crime legislation is thus often unable to get to what is often the core of what causes hate crime by itself, and efforts to get at that core pose a risk to the functioning of whatever democratic values we hold dear. The solution, as such, should be two-fold, for one, we should increase our efforts of calling out hate speech whenever it is present, drown out such speech from public spaces and report such speech in private spaces, make it difficult for the toxic ideas presented in that speech from infesting and motivating others. Secondly, we must educate and inform as many people as possible of the common characteristics of hate speech and the common ways it can spread, and reform and teach those convicted of hate crimes of techniques and strategies that may reduce *their* hatred.

A BRIEF HISTORY OF HATE (AND ITS DISCONTENTS)

The United States has a sordid history with hate, and it has provoked it through both state and non-state means. Slavery, the brutal massacres and genocides of Indigenous people, the illegalization of homosexuality and queerness in general, were advanced through a tandem acceptance between the government and the public that it was *right* to hate and discriminate against an "other." The Civil Rights Acts of the 1960's changed this model but did not fully confront the depth of bitter hatred that the state itself helped to invoke for centuries. The steady stream of federal hate crime laws since, such as Title I of 1968 Civil Rights Act"[1] the Violent Crime Control and Law Enforcement Act of 1994,[2] and the Matthew Shepard and James Byrd Jr. Hate Crimes Prevention Ac,[3] alleviate, but even by their own measure fail to fully confront hate crime.

These laws, only meant towards *federal* crimes, left the great majority of hate crime-oriented work to the states. The effort to create state statutes against hate crimes began in the early 1980's, with Washington and Oregon putting the first resolutions in place in 1981 (Shively, 2005). States have steadily introduced and reformed hate crime statutes ever since. Work has been continual in implementing new characteristics that would be protected under hate crime laws, with gender and sexuality often being recent characteristics added onto hate crime statutes. Furthermore, coordination between federal and state governments, driven by the Hate Crime Statistics Act of 1990, have sharpened data collection efforts regarding hate crimes considerably.

HATRED AND ENFORCEMENT

However, the unequal distribution of hate crime measures and identities covered under hate crime law have led to an uneven patchwork of enforcement regarding hate crimes. Ohio, for instance, has no statute covering discrimination against sexuality. Other states, such as Indiana, list no characteristics at all, making enforcement incredibly vague. Furthermore, the states of Arkansas, North Dakota, South Carolina, and Wyoming have no hate crime statute whatsoever, making data collection all the more difficult and enforcement essentially non-existent for non-federal related crimes.[4] Even in states with generally complete hate-crime statutes, different local situations vary enforcement and reporting immensely, and that often comes down to individuals trusting the authorities to hear their statements and respond accordingly—trust that has often been negligible in recent times. Hate crime statutes, as such, can lead authorities to awkwardly confront a social situation they helped make.

Enforcement against hate crimes, then, not only is incomplete, but also fundamentally rests on problematic grounds, many groups have justifiable reasons why they do not want to report to the authorities

---

[1] This legislation never explicitly says "hate crime" in its language, potentially because "hate crime" as a term did not really exist yet. It does take on many of the common attributes of hate crime legislation as it makes it it a federal crime to "by force or threat of force willfully injures, intimidates or interferes with or attempts to injure, intimidate or interfere with" anyone from a listed set of federally protected activities "because of (their) race, color, religion or national origin." Such language is consistent with modern language concerning hate crimes that it was revamped during the passing Matthew Shepard and James Byrd Jr. Hate Crimes Prevention Act (See footnote three for more information on that legislation) to be a "hate crime" law.

[2] This legislation required the United States Sentencing Commission to increase penalties for hate crimes committed on the basis of the actual or perceived "race color religion, national origin, ethnicity, or gender of any person."

[3] This legislation, importantly, removed the prerequisites set by the 1968 act that the victim of a hate crime must be engaging in a "federally protected activity" and added in crimes motivated by a victim's actual or perceived, gender, sexual orientation, gender identity, or disability."

[4] South Carolina and Arkansas have statutes criminalizing or giving penalty enhancements for vandalizing places of worship, but no specific statute that lists characteristics.

about their strife, despite it perhaps being in their best interest. Efforts to "increase enforcement" will not change this fact. A change to this would require both a *political* response, and an *anti-political*—or non-profit based— response. A political response would require states and the federal government to adopt measures that would increase the equity of all, and measures that reduce the necessity of the police on all fronts. Some of these are rather optimistic goals, which leaves the *anti-political* response a necessary one in the meantime. This would continue the profusion of non-profit organizations into the sphere of hate crime work, allowing them to address whatever trauma has occurred, and act as a liaison between the victim and the various systems and institutions they must navigate to get justice.

CONCLUSION

In conclusion, the emergence of hate crime laws, while an important and inspiring narrative in a country which has so much baggage when it comes to hatred and discrimination, should not be considered a panacea when it comes to dealing with discrimination in this country. The key difficulty of hate crime statutes is that they graft what is ultimately a *legal* solution onto what is essentially a larger *political* problem, and they will always be limited in that sense. This does not mean that hate crime statutes should be thrown-out, on the contrary, they hold an important place on the frontlines against hatred in this country when nothing else works; however, the continued proliferation and increase in hate crimes across the country show the natural limitations of such law, and our generally lackluster efforts in fighting hatred in other areas. If we are to decrease hatred in these times of intense polarization and political tension, we must begin by understanding and addressing hate in a more holistic way.

IDEA - Read in a circle of friends and family silently or have one person read it aloud. When you're done take some time to digest what he says and discuss your reactions.

The Ballot or the Bullet
Malcolm X
April 3, 1964
Cleveland, Ohio

© Natata/Shutterstock.com

IMPORTANT FACTS AND TERMS

Ableism: A set of beliefs or practices at the individual, community, or systemic level that devalue and discriminate against people with physical, intellectual, or psychiatric disabilities and often rests on the assumption that disabled people need to be 'fixed' in one form or the other.

Accessibility: The extent to which a space is readily approachable and usable by people with disabilities. A space can be described as a physical or literal space, such as a facility, website, conference room, office, or bathroom, or a figurative space, such as a conversation or activity.

Affirm: To acknowledge, respect, value, and support someone's full identity and self—including race, ethnicity, sexual orientation, gender identity and expression, experiences, ideas, beliefs, etc.—and to encourage the development and exploration of who they are.

Anti-Black Racism: Any attitude, behavior, practice, or policy that explicitly or implicitly reflects the belief that Black people are inferior to another racial group. Anti-Black racism is reflected in interpersonal, institutional, and systemic levels of racism and is a function of White supremacy.

Anti-Racism Active process of identifying and challenging racism, by changing systems, organizational structures, policies and practices, and attitudes, to redistribute power in an equitable manner.

Cisgender: Someone who identifies with the gender/sex that they were assigned at birth.

Classism: The institutional, cultural, and individual set of practices and beliefs that assign differential value to people according to their socioeconomic status. Classism also refers to the systematic oppression of poor and working class people by those who control resources.

Color-Blind Racial Ideology: The belief that people should be regarded and treated as equally as possible, without regard to race or ethnicity. While a color-blind racial ideology may seem to be a pathway to achieve equity, in reality it invalidates the importance of peoples' culture; ignores the manifestations of racist policies which preserves the ongoing processes that maintain racial and ethnic stratification in social institutions.

Colorism: Using White skin color as the standard, colorism is the allocation of privilege and favor to lighter skin colors and disadvantage to darker skin colors. Colorism operates both within and across racial and ethnic groups.

Cultural Humility: When one maintains an interpersonal stance that is open to individuals and communities of varying cultures, in relation to aspects of the cultural identity most important to the person. Cultural humility can include a life-long commitment to self-critique about differences in culture and a commitment to be aware of and actively mitigate power imbalances between cultures.

Culture: The languages, customs, beliefs, rules, arts, knowledge, and collective identities and memories developed by members of all social groups that make their social environments meaningful.

Discrimination: The unequal treatment of members of various groups based on race, ethnicity, gender, gender expression, socioeconomic class, sexual orientation, physical or mental ability, religion, citizenship status, a combination of those identified, and/or other categories.

Diversity: A synonym for variety. A diversity focus emphasizes "how many of these" we have in the room, organization, etc. Diversity programs and cultural celebrations/education programs are not equivalent to racial justice or inclusion. It is possible to name, acknowledge, and celebrate diversity without doing anything to transform the institutional or structural systems that produce, and maintain, racialized injustices in our communities.

Equity: The effort to provide different levels of support based on an individual's or group's needs in order to achieve fairness in outcomes. Working to achieve equity acknowledges unequal starting places and the need to correct the imbalance.

Ethnicity: Denotes groups that share a common identity-based ancestry, language, or culture. It is often based on religion, beliefs, and customs as well as memories of migration or colonization

Freedom of Information Act (FOIA): The Freedom of Information Act (FOIA) was enacted in 1966 and gives American citizens the right to access any federal documents, except those that are protected from public disclosure by one of nine exemptions or three special law enforcement exclusions.

Gender Pronoun: The term one uses to identify themselves in place of their name (i.e. ze/hir/hirs, ey/em/eirs, they/them/theirs, she/her/hers, he/him/his, etc.). The use of the specific gender pronoun identified by each individual should be respected and should not be regarded as optional.

Homophobia: The fear and hatred of or discomfort with people who are attracted to members of the same gender. Homophobia occurs in a broader heterosexist social context that systematically disadvantages LGBTQ+ people and promotes and rewards anti-LGBTQ+ sentiment.

Implicit Bias: A belief or attitude that affects our understanding, decision, and actions, and that exists without our conscious awareness.

Inclusion: A state of belonging, when persons of different backgrounds and identities are valued, integrated, and welcomed equitably as decision-makers and collaborators. Inclusion involves people being given the opportunity to grow and feel/know they belong. Diversity efforts alone do not create inclusive environments. Inclusion involves a sense of coming as you are and being accepted, rather than feeling the need to assimilate.

Indigenous Decolonization: The repatriation of Indigenous land and life, as well as the ongoing theoretical and political processes used to contest and reframe narratives about indigenous community histories and the effects of colonial expansion, genocide, and cultural assimilation. Indigenous people engaged in decolonization work adopt a critical stance towards White, western-centric practices and discourse and seek to reposition knowledge within Indigenous cultural practices. This is commonly referred to as decolonization.

Institutional/Systemic Racism: The practices that perpetuate racial disparities, uphold White supremacy, and serve to the detriment and harm of persons of color and keep them in negative cycles. Institutional/systemic racism also refers to policies that generate different outcomes for persons of different race. These laws, policies, and practices are not necessarily explicit in mentioning any racial group, but work to create advantages for White persons and disadvantages for people of color.

Internalized Racism: The conscious and unconscious development of ideas, beliefs, actions, and behaviors that demonstrate one's acceptance of the dominant society's racist tropes and stereotypes about their own race. Internalized racism is the simultaneous hating of oneself and/or one's own race and valuing of the dominant race. Internalized racism is an individual's system of oppression in response to any and all forms of racism.

Interpersonal Racism: The racism that occurs between individuals. It is when someone consciously or unconsciously employs or acts upon on racist thoughts, in ways that perpetuate stereotypes and harms people of color. See: Individual/ Personal Racism; Implicit Bias.

Intersectionality: Coined by Professor Kimberlé Crenshaw in 1989, this term describes the ways in which race, class, gender, and other aspects of our identity "intersect" overlap and interact with one another, informing the way in which individuals simultaneously experience oppression and privilege in their daily lives interpersonally and systemically. Intersectionality promotes the idea that aspects of our identity do not work in a silo. Intersectionality, then, provides a basis for understanding how these individual identity markers work with one another.

Justice: The process required to move us from an unfair, unequal, or inequitable state to one which is fair, equal, or equitable, depending on the specific content. Justice is a transformative practice that relies on the entire community to respond to past and current harm when it occurs in society. Through justice, we seek a proactive enforcement of policies, practices and attitudes that produce equitable access, opportunities, treatment and outcomes for all regardless of the various identities that one holds.

Law: A statement that dictates an individual, business, country, or nation's conduct and can be rein-forced through a monetary fine or prison if defied.

LGBTQ+: An acronym for "lesbian, gay, bisexual, transgender, and queer." The plus (+) is inclusive of all other expressions of gender identity and sexual-orientation. Liberation The progression toward or the conscious or unconscious state of being in which one can freely exist, think, dream, and thrive in a way which operates outside of traditional systems of oppression. Liberation acknowledges history, but does not bind any person to disparate systems or outcomes. Liberation is a culture of solidarity, respect, and dignity.

Marginalization: The process that occurs when members of a dominant group relegate a particular group to the edge of society by not allowing them an active voice, identity, or place for the purpose of maintaining power.

Misgender: To intentionally or unintentionally refer to a person, relate to a person, or use language to describe a person that does not align with their gender identity. This often occurs when people make assumptions about a person's gender.

Oppression: A system of supremacy and discrimination for the benefit of a limited dominant class that perpetuates itself through differential treatment, ideological domination, and institutional control. Oppression reflects the inequitable distribution of current and historical structural and institutional power, where a socially constructed binary of a "dominant group" horde power, wealth, and resources at the detriment of the many. This creates a lack of access, opportunity, safety, security, and resources for non-dominant populations.

Othering: The perception or placing of a person or a group outside and/or in opposition to what is considered to be the norm. Othering is based on a conscious or unconscious assumption that a certain identified group poses a threat to the favored or dominant group. See: Marginalization.

Patriarchy: The manifestation and institutionalization of men and/or masculinity as dominant over women and/or femininity in both the private and public spheres, such as the home, political, religious, and social institutions, sports, etc. Patriarchy is deeply connected with cissexism and heterosexism through the perpetuation and enforcement of the gender binary.

Privileges and immunities clause: A clause of Article IV, Section 2 of the Constitution that allows any American citizen fundamental rights and that discrimination cannot be a legitimate reason to deprive any American citizen their rights. Of course, slaves were not considered whole people (see "Three-Fifths Compromise," which dictated that slaves were only considered three-fifths of the population), so this clause did not apply to African-Americans until the Civil Rights movement. Arguably, this is still a topic up for debate.

Racial Microaggression: Commonplace verbal, behavioral, or environmental indignities, whether intentional or unintentional, that communicate or imply hostile or derogatory racial slights and insults toward people of color (e.g. asking a person of color "How did you get your job?" to imply they are not qualified).

Racially Coded Language: Language that is seemingly race-neutral but is actually a disguise for racial stereotypes without the stigma of explicit racism.

Racism: The systematic subjugation of members of targeted racial groups, who hold less socio-political power and/or are racialized as non-White, as means to uphold White supremacy. Racism differs from prejudice, hatred, or discrimination because it requires one racial group to have systematic power and superiority over other groups in society. Often, racism is supported and maintained, both implicitly and explicitly, by institutional structures and policies, cultural norms and values, and individual behaviors.

Roe v. Wade: A 1971 Supreme Court case that made it legal for women to seek an abortion, regardless of if it is for personal or medical reasons. Previously, few states would grant an abortion and it was only if the pregnancy would endanger the woman's life.

Seditious libel: A law that punishes anyone who criticizes or lies about the government, effectively stifling the First Amendment and making it difficult for certain, subversive opinions to be made public. This law makes it difficult to open a dialogue about troublesome governmental issues in many media outlets for fear of punishment.

Sexual orientation: A term used to describe the gender or genders of the people to whom one is sexually attracted to. Some common examples include heterosexual or straight, gay, lesbian, bisexual, pansexual, asexual, and queer

Social Justice: A process, not an outcome, which (1) seeks fair (re)distribution of resources, opportunities, and responsibilities; (2) challenges the roots of oppression and injustice; (3) empowers all people to exercise self-determination and realize their full potential; (4) and builds social solidarity and community capacity for collaborative action.

SOGIE: An acronym that was created by the United Nations to honor the fluidity of numerous and ever expanding identities related to sexual orientation (SO), gender identity (GI), and expression (E).

Substantive due process: The limitations placed on the subject matter of a state or federal law, as dictated by the due process clauses of the Fifth and Fourteenth Amendments of the Constitution.

Suffrage: A woman's right to vote. The women's suffrage movement took place in the late-nineenth century and early-twentieth century, resulting in the Nineteenth Amendment passing in 1920.

Webster v. Reproductive Health Services: A 1986 Supreme Court case wherein Reproductive Health Services and other abortion services filed suit against the Missouri legislature, which had recently passed a law dictating that state money could not be used to fund abortion facilities and that a viability test was necessary at twenty-weeks in the pregnancy. They argued that the law violated the Roe v. Wade ruling. The Supreme Court found that the Missouri law did not violate Roe v. Wade and was constitutional.

White Fragility: A range of defensive (and centering) emotions and behaviors that White people exhibit when confronted with uncomfortable truths about race. This may include outward displays of emotions such as anger, fear, and guilt, and behaviors such as argumentation, silence, and leaving the stress-inducing situation. These behaviors, in turn, function to reinstate White racial equilibrium.

White Privilege: The unearned power and advantages that benefit people just by virtue of being White or being perceived as White. See: White Fragility; White Supremacy.

White Supremacy: An institutionally perpetuated and ever-evolving system of exploitation and domination that consolidates and maintains power and resources among White people. This system promotes the ideology of Whiteness as the standard and the belief that White people are superior to other races.

Xenophobia: Any attitude, behavior, practice, or policy that explicitly or implicitly reflects the belief that immigrants are inferior to the dominant group of people. Xenophobia is reflected in interpersonal, institutional, and systemic levels of oppression and is a function of White supremacy.

Chapter 7

IMMIGRATION

The US is again increasingly a nation of immigrants.

Fourteen percent of people in the US in 2019 were foreign-born, up from a low of 5% in 1970 and near the high of 15% in the early 1900s.

https://usafacts.org/state-of-the-union/immigration/

CRIME & JUSTICE

The total prison population decreased 11% between the 2009 peak and 2019, with decreases in federal, California, and New York state prison populations accounting for 45% of the decline.

Federal prison populations declined 16% in the same period and California and New York's both decreased 23%.

https://usafacts.org/state-of-the-union/crime/

CRIME & JUSTICE

Firearm deaths increased 18% from 2014 to 2018, accounting for 1.4% of all deaths in that time.

There were nearly 40,000 firearm deaths in 2018, more of which were suicides than homicides.

https://usafacts.org/state-of-the-union/crime/

ENVIRONMENT & ENERGY

2020 was the second-warmest year on record.

In 2020, the average global temperature was 0.98 °C (1.76 °F) above the 20th-century average. It was also 0.02 °C (0.04 °F) below 2016, the warmest year on record.

https://usafacts.org/state-of-the-union/energy-environment/

References

American Humanist Association (2021) About. Retrieved from https://americanhumanist.org/about/
Chambliss, W. (1989). State Organized Crime – The American Society of Criminology, 1988 Presidential Address. *Criminology 27*(2),183–208.
Freccero, C. (1999). Popular Culture: An Introduction. New York: NYU Press
Young, I. (1988). The Five Faces Of Oppression. *Philosophical Forum*. 19: 270–290.

CHAPTER EIGHT

Legislating Change: States Rights and Congressional Lawmaking

© Morphart Creation/Shutterstock.com

The Constitution divides the federal government into three branches to ensure a central government in which no individual or group gains too much control:

Legislative—Makes laws (Congress)

Executive—Carries out laws (President, Vice President, and Cabinet)

Judicial—Evaluates laws (Supreme Court and other courts)

The legislative branch enacts legislation, confirms or rejects presidential appointments, and has the authority to declare war. This branch comprises Congress (the Senate and House of Representatives) and several agencies that provide support services to Congress.

The legislative process in the United States is designed to allow for our representative democracy to give the people a voice in the law-making process. The population of each state determines how many seats in the House of Representatives they have.

According to the U.S. House of Representatives, Laws begin as ideas. First, a representative sponsors a bill. The bill is then assigned to a committee for study. If released by the committee, the bill is put on a calendar to be voted on, debated or amended. If the bill passes by simple majority (218 of 435), the bill moves to the Senate. In the Senate, the bill is assigned to another committee and, if released, debated and voted on. Again, a simple majority (51 of 100) passes the bill. Finally, a conference committee made of House and Senate members works out any differences between the House and Senate versions of the bill. The resulting bill returns to the House and Senate for final approval. The Government Printing Office prints the revised bill in a process called enrolling. The President has 10 days to sign or veto the enrolled bill.

The American political system has developed a discourse that includes the notion of states rates, which allows for political powers to be held by states governments rather than only the federal government. It's a shared model that basically allows the states to pass their own laws and enforce them as long as they do not breach federal law, these are described in the constitution as concurrent powers and the rights of the states as reserved powers. These powers are enumerated in the U.S. Constitution in the Tenth amendment.

All 50 states have legislatures made up of elected representatives, who consider matters brought forth by the governor or introduced by its members to create legislation that becomes law. The legislature also approves a state's budget and initiates tax legislation and articles of impeachment. The latter is part of a system of checks and balances among the three branches of government that mirrors the federal system and prevents any branch from abusing its power.

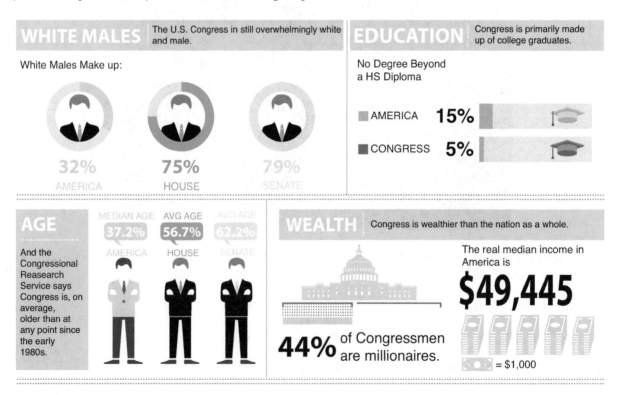

Does Congress look like America?

Source: Adapted from yes magazine
https://www.yesmagazine.org/education/2016/09/15/infographic-does-congress-look-like-america

Every state except one has a bicameral legislature made up of two chambers: a smaller upper house and a larger lower house. Together the two chambers make state laws and fulfill other governing responsibilities. The smaller upper chamber is always called the Senate, and its members generally serve longer terms, usually 4 years. The larger lower chamber is most often called the House of Representatives but some states call it the Assembly or the House of Delegates. Its members usually serve shorter terms, often 2 years. Nebraska is the lone state that has just one chamber in its legislature.

STATES RIGHTS AND DRUG LAWS

A recent example that shows the of this are the rule changes around the use of marijuana medicinally and recreationally.

Five forms of marijuana legalization have been implemented across the country. Marijuana is treated like alcohol. Marijuana use is legal for adults 21 and older for any and all purposes, including medical and recreational uses. All government-enforced penalties for using and possessing pot for personal use are removed. The amount of cannabis one may possess and grow varies by state; large quantities generally remain illegal.

Voters in Arizona, Montana, New Jersey, and South Dakota have approved measures to regulate cannabis for adult recreational use. Legalization of marijuana use does not always mean it's legal to purchase. In Washington, DC, it's legal for anyone 21 and older to possess up to two ounces of DC weed, grow up to six marijuana plants in the district (with up to three in the mature flowering stage), and gift up to an ounce of marijuana to anyone 21 years or older—as long as no sales or trades occur. This is because it is not legal to buy marijuana in DC. Instead, consumers buy seemingly overpriced stickers and receive the marijuana product—the object of the transaction—as a "gift with purchase."

Medicinal allows doctors to recommend marijuana for a wide range of conditions, including pain, nausea, depression, anxiety, and PTSD. States determine the medical conditions for which physicians can prescribe cannabis and cannabinoids. In a few states, medical cannabis laws are lax enough to be functionally like full legalization; in others, medical cannabis is strictly regulated.

In addition to the 15 states plus DC with legalized recreational marijuana, 19 states have legalized only the medical use of cannabis with a doctor's recommendation. Alabama recently passed a medicinal marijuana law in May 2021. When implemented, it will be the 16th state to allow medicinal use only. If the South Dakota high court decides in favor of voters, the state will implement a medical marijuana program on July 1, 2021. Six states allow marijuana to be used for medicinal purposes but do not allow it to be smoked.

Decriminalization eliminates jail or prison time for limited possession of marijuana, though other penalties may remain in place. Some states treat minor marijuana offenses like minor traffic infractions—violators are punished with fines of a few hundred dollars. Other states with decriminalization laws may still include possible jail time for possessing larger amounts of marijuana, selling marijuana, or trafficking marijuana.

As of April 13, 2021, 27 states and DC have decriminalized marijuana (this includes states that have legalized recreational pot and medicinal pot).

Even in states that have decriminalized marijuana, possessing larger quantities or selling cannabis may still carry significant penalties.

Recreational marijuana is legal in 16 states and Washington, DC.

Fully legal   Mixed legally   Recreational legality pending   Fully illegal

Adapted from USA Facts

Source: State governments

THE 2020 CENSUS AND SHIFTS IN CONGRESS

The Census Bureau made the official 2020 state population numbers public on April 26. With that release came reapportionment, which uses a formula to redistribute each state's share of the 435 House of Representative seats starting in the 2022 midterm election. That formula takes state population into account. The changes in apportionment will have a political effect, notably in the Electoral College, where states are allotted electoral votes based on the number of members in Congress.

WHICH STATES GAINED AND LOST SEATS

In addition to Texas gaining two seats, five states gained one seat: Colorado, Florida, Oregon, Montana, and North Carolina. Seven states lost seats: California, Illinois, Michigan, New York, Ohio, Pennsylvania, and West Virginia.

The electoral map changes with reapportionment. The congressional seats apportioned in the census count have a direct impact on the presidential electoral process, where each state has an electoral vote for each of its members of the House and its two Senators. (The exception is Washington, DC, which has three electoral votes but does not participate in reapportionment or have voting members in Congress.)

Every state must adhere to the Voting Rights Act for redistricting, ensuring each district has approximately the same population. The shapes of these districts are redrawn using population data provided by the Census Bureau that includes summary information of racial and ethnic breakdowns and the number of people living in group quarters like prisons.

While this piece primarily addresses congressional redistricting, the same data are used to redraw state legislative districts. Many states have constitutional or legal guidelines for what they must consider in drawing congressional districts. Among the considerations:

- Thirty-three states require geographically "compact" districts.
- Thirty-seven states require that all land in the districts be "contiguous."
- Thirty-three states require that districts not separate political subdivisions like counties unless necessary.
- Twenty-three require districts to consider "communities of interest," which could include everything from racially alike groups or socioeconomically alike groups.

LEGISLATURE-BASED

© Rob Crandall/Shutterstock.com

In most states, the state legislature has authority over the drawing and approval of maps. In some states, the new districts are approved via regular legislation and subject to a governor's veto. In others, like Connecticut and North Carolina, the maps are not subject to governor's approval.

Next year, 17 states will have maps drawn in Republican-controlled legislatures and approved by a Republican governor.

Eight states will draw maps in Democrat-controlled legislatures where either there is a Democratic governor or the maps will not be subject to gubernatorial veto.

Independent Commission

Nine states will have an independent commission create maps not subject to legislative approval: Arizona, California, Colorado, Hawaii, Idaho, Michigan, Montana, New Jersey, and Washington. (Montana had a single seat before the census; it gained a second seat following reapportionment.)

Some content from: https://usafacts.org/articles/reapportionment-and-redistricting-after-the-2020-census-explained/

ACCOUNTABILITY

Impeachment—The House of Representatives has the ability to impeach government officials, as if they were the "prosecutors" of the government. The Senate has tried 17 federal officials, including 2 presidents since 1789.

Expulsion—Each house of Congress (as explained in Article I, Section 5) can punish members by expelling them from Congress by a two-thirds vote. This has only happened 15 times.

Censure—This is a form of punishment in the form of being expelled within the Senate. Since 1789, the Senate has censured nine of its members.

Investigations—This is a primary role of Congressional oversight. If there are occurrences where Congress feels like they need to investigate, they can hold various branches of government accountable through investigation, but other bodies and people are subject to investigation.

Contested Senate Elections—The U.S. Constitution gives each house of Congress the power to be the "judges" on election, returns, and qualification of its own members (Article I, Section 5).

RULE-MAKING

Treaties—The U.S. Constitution gives the Senate the ability to vote on and approve treaties that come from the executive branch. The Senate needs a two-thirds vote.

The Senate can amend or make changes to the treaty. As a part of the balance of power, there are some executive agreements with foreign nations that the president can make without the Senate's approval.

Filibuster and Cloture—Filibuster is meant to stop debate on an issue and stall a vote. This has been in practice since 1850. There was unlimited debate allowed until 1917, when the Senate adopted Rule 22 that gave the Senate permission to end a debate with a two-thirds vote. In 1975, this was reduced to three-fifths (60 of the 100 member senate).

NOMINATIONS FOR APPOINTMENTS

Nominations—One of the Senate's major powers lies in their ability to confirm or deny nominations for major political offices in the US government. As stated in Article 2, Section 2 President "shall nominate, by and with the Advice and Consent of the Senate, shall appoint Ambassadors, other public Ministers and Consuls, Judges of the Supreme Court, and all other Officers of the United States."

FIRST IN THE HOUSE AND THE SENATE

The powers outlined in the Constitution provide the citizens with a range of representation. Those who are elected to represent us in the first House was assembled in New York in 1789 and was later moved to Philadelphia in 1790 and then to Washington, DC in 1800.

POWERS OF CONGRESS AND THE BANK BAILOUTS

During the Great Recession of 2008, more than 8 million people lost their jobs. Homes were foreclosing and businesses were shutting down left and right, leaving families homeless and severely crippling the small business market.

Throughout all of the economic disaster that took place between 2007 and 2009, making this past recession comparable to, and maybe worse than, the Great Depression of the 1930s, there was quite a bit of debate about what exactly started the Recession. For approximately 20 years, the United States had been racking up massive debts due to the Iraq and Afghanistan Wars; the government was practically hemorrhaging money to pay for these oil wars and it was certainly taking its toll on the country's economic stability. However, once people started to follow the money and the paper trail, though the government's gross misuse of taxpayer money was certainly an irritant to the bloated debt problem, it came down to banks and private lenders offering housing loans that eventually broke the economy.

Between 2004 and 2006, banks and lenders were essentially loaning out houses by offering loans at a remarkably low interest rate. Eventually, this led to the subprime mortgage crisis that crippled the economy because, suddenly, there was more money being loaned than was being paid back to the banks. As such, many lenders and banks found themselves in an awkward predicament of needing to borrow money in order to keep themselves afloat. Many banks were forced to declare bankruptcy or were acquired. In 2008, after almost voting against it, the House of Representatives voted to approve a $700 billion bailout package. This bailout would allow the Treasury to buy out any financial mistakes that banks and other financial institutions made during the time leading up to the Recession. The bailout essentially placed a bandage on a larger economic wound that will never be completely healed as long as the government believes that the only way to solve an economic problem is to throw more money at it, especially considering that the people they bailed out were the people who were responsible for the economic downturn in the first place.

Meanwhile, welfare, education, and environmental budgets have been getting cut extensively. The House of Representatives were also pressured by the Senate to push the vote toward the bailout. As a result, the Democrat representatives are hoping to tighten economic controls on corporations to prevent another similar economic catastrophe. However, this promise is in a murky water of being ignored when bad behavior and decisions were rewarded with essentially handing over taxpayer money to rectify a mistake that they had already paid for in high unemployment rates and difficulty re-entering the job market.

The Confirmation of B. Kavanaugh

IMPORTANT FACTS AND TERMS

Bicameralism: The Congress as it is broken into two chambers, the House of Representatives and the Senate. This allows for each district of a state to have a national representative based on population, for the House of Representatives, and for each state to have two national Senators.

Enumerated powers: Thirty to 35 powers listed in Article I, Section 8 of the Constitution that dictates the powers that Congress has in the United States.

Impeachment: The process by which a president or other high ranking official is found guilty or innocent of a particular crime, often treason or bribery. Contrary to popular opinion, the impeachment process does not necessarily mean that the individual has to leave office.

Senatorial courtesy: The Senate practice of only appointing a presidential nominee if it is approved by both of the appointee's senators or by the senior senator of the president's party.

Separation of powers: A term used to describe the government being separated into the executive, legislative, and judicial branches to avoid any one branch of government having omnipotent power and the ability to prevent the actions of another branch.

Veto power: The Constitutional right that one branch of government has to refuse approval for another branch of government to carry out any action. This particular power has been responsible for many governmental standstills regarding important issues.

War Powers Resolution: Requires the President to consult with Congress regarding acts of war, including declaring war or deploying troops to any given combat situation.

CHAPTER NINE

The Realities and Misgivings of Presidential Power

© Drop of Light/Shutterstock.com

The President has a difficult job in America. The President serves as the head of the executive branch of the American Government and, no matter how little people know about politics, in general, the consensus is that the President has more on his or her plate than any one person should have to deal with.

The executive branch carries out and enforces laws. It includes the president, vice president, the Cabinet, executive departments, independent agencies, and other boards, commissions, and committees.

American citizens have the right to vote for the president and vice president through free, confidential ballots.

Key roles of the executive branch include:

- President—The president leads the country. He or she is the head of state, leader of the federal government, and Commander in Chief of the United States armed forces. The president serves a 4-year term and can be elected no more than two times.
- Vice president—The vice president supports the president. If the president is unable to serve, the vice president becomes president. The vice president can be elected and serve an unlimited number of 4-year terms as vice president, even under a different president.
- The Cabinet—Cabinet members serve as advisors to the president. They include the vice president, heads of executive departments, and other high-ranking government officials. Cabinet members are nominated by the president and must be approved by a simple majority of the Senate—51 votes if all 100 Senators vote.

Vice President Kamala Harris

Presidents are responsible for negotiating with international powers during times of peace and conflict, serving as the Commander in Chief of the military, enforcing or vetoing laws that Congress creates, and appointing heads of and chairing the President's Cabinet, among other things. However, there are certain aspects of the executive branch that seems to overlap the judicial and Congressional branches enough that there is confusion over who is actually responsible for what aspects of the government that are failing. With the recent election of Donald Trump, we have seen some ways that presidential power can be expressed.

https://usafacts.org/data/topics/people-society/democracy-and-society/

Since there seems to be a morbid affair with our government viewing corporations as individuals, we will pretend for a second that America is a corporation and that the President is the CEO of that company. More often than not, the CEO is in charge of overseeing the operations of the company but may not necessarily be directly responsible for every action that occurs. Logistically speaking that would not be possible because the CEO is only one person and is not capable of being in more than one place at any given time.

No matter how powerful someone is, physics does not work that way. The difference between the CEO in this metaphor and the President in the United States is public exposure. A CEO has the questionable privilege to be relatively anonymous in many ways; the President does not have that option. Because the President is often the face and the voice of the United States, anything that goes wrong in America is often blamed on him or her. President Trump has a business background. Some have speculated that his business skills may not work as well within a government environment. This raises the question—What should we require our presidential candidates, and the presidents we elect, to know about how the system works and the people they represent?

While the saying goes that when someone in lower management makes a mistake, it is executive management's mistake, it also means that people who want to hold government accountable for its foibles often direct their ire at the wrong person. Often, it is Congress who we need to be held accountable. The recent scandal over Russian involvement in swaying the 2016 election. There is a current investigation into these allegations by Congress. Unfortunately, we have a Congress member Rep. Nunes who could have been involved or had knowledge of information that he is now responsible to investigate. These are where we see gaps in common-sense judgment.

The President's powers are mitigated by the constitution. As are all branches of government. Each branch was designed to make the powerful in government work with one another.

The disadvantages to the separation of powers in the government are numerous. As mentioned, it means that when the public wants to correct any problem that they see in their government, they have to go through different bureaucratic channels, or they have the problem of not knowing who to address with their concerns. However, the separation of powers means that no one branch of government has the power to write and enforce laws without another branch signing off on it as the President does with laws that Congress passes. Our Judicial Branch could step in and deem an act of the legislative or executive branch unconstitutional. In theory, this was meant to avoid corruption and monarchical rule in America, under the auspices of protecting our democracy.

Most of the government has been elite white men and especially at this point in government, most have come from families of wealth and power. Therefore, no matter how much they check and balance the bills, laws, and reforms, there will always be a difference between what they think will happen after the different laws are passed and what actually happens for the rest of us.

The cost–benefit analysis always comes up short between what they think will be necessary sacrifices and what will be catastrophic consequences for their constituents. Although President Obama came from humble beginnings and, being the first African American President certainly changes the game, there is still a divide between what he allows to happen in the government and what his constituents actually want to happen. The very nature of the presidency is that he or she is not going to be in direct contact with those who elected him or her, except during the campaign. That does not mean that there is a cognitive connection, aside from memorizing talking points. On the other end of the spectrum, there are the moments when the public realizes that the President is abusing her or his power and demands that there be punishment for his or her actions. However, throughout American history, only two presidents have ever been impeached: Andrew Johnson in 1868 for high crimes and misdemeanors and President Clinton in 1998 for perjury and obstruction of justice.

The impeachment process, while often assumed to mean that the President is required to step down from office, only means that he has been charged with a high crime, often treason, bribery, or another related crime. However, considering that President Clinton was impeached for an affair while President Bush was allowed to continue his presidency through two terms despite blatant war crimes against humanity, the process has its flaws.

The House of Representatives holds a vote for impeachment that only requires a minority vote, then the hearings are held in the Senate.

The idea that impeachment is a possibility shows that the American people do have the option to pressure Congress to seek just leadership in the executive branch.

This section delves into what powers the President has in office, what he or she agrees to do when in office, how the impeachment process works, and how to direct grievances through the proper channels so that there are no hold-ups through the bureaucratic minefield that the government has placed to halt progress and change. Presidential powers are expressed in three major ways. The first way is through their responsibility to maintain economic growth within our capitalist system.

This involves utilizing the resources of the executive branch to sustain economic growth and stability. Secondly, the President works to defend America's political interests domestically and abroad. This responsibility asks the President to protect Americans from attack and in most cases, to uphold and maintain American social, economic, or political dominance. The third way that the President is able to express her power is by maintaining political stability as Commander in Chief of the military. Doing so includes the government's administrative concerns, financial accountability, and the use of military resources.

PRESIDENTIAL CABINET DEPARTMENT REPRESENTATION

Vice President of the United States, Department of State http://www.state.gov
Department of the Treasury http://www.treasury.gov
Department of Defense http://www.defense.gov
Department of Justice http://www.usdoj.gov
Department of the Interior http://www.doi.gov Department of Agriculture http://www.usda.gov
    Department of Commerce http://www.commerce.gov
Department of Labor http://www.dol.gov
Department of Health and Human Services, http://www.hhs.gov Department of Housing and Urban
    Development http://www.hud.gov Department of Transportation http://www.dot.gov
Department of Energy http://www.energy.gov Department of Education http://www.ed.gov
    Department of Veterans Affairs http://www.va.gov Department of Homeland Security http://
    www.dhs.gov White House Chief of Staff

Environmental Protection Agency http://www.epa.gov
Office of Management & Budget whitehouse.gov/omb
United States Trade Representative www.ustr.gov
United States Mission to the United Nations usun.state.gov/
Council of Economic Advisers www.whitehouse.gov/administration/eop/cea/ Small Business
    Administration www.sba.gov/

THE UNITED STATES GOVERNMENT

The Constitution

LEGISLATIVE BRANCH	EXECUTIVE BRANCH	JUDICIAL BRANCH
THE CONGRESS	THE PRESIDENT	THE SUPREME COURT OF
SENATE | HOUSE	THE VICE PRESIDENT	THE UNITED STATES
100 Senators	EXECUTIVE OFFICE OF THE PRESIDENT	9 Justices
435 Representatives Architect of the Capitol United States Botanic Garden Government Accountability Office Government Printing Office Library of Congress Congressional Budget Office US Capitol Police	15 Cabinet Members White House Office Office of the Vice President Council of Economic Advisers Council on Environmental Quality National Security Council Office of Administration Office of Management and Budget Office of National Drug Control Policy Office of Policy Development Office of Science and Technology Policy Office of the US Trade Representative	United States Courts of Appeals United States District Courts Territorial Courts United States Court of International Trade United States Court of Federal Claims Administrative Office of the United States Courts Federal Judicial Center United States Sentencing Commission

Significant Reporting Entities (15)

DEPARTMENT OF AGRICULTURE	DEPARTMENT OF COMMERCE	DEPARTMENT OF DEFENSE	DEPARTMENT OF EDUCATION	DEPARTMENT OF ENERGY
DEPARTMENT OF HEALTH AND HUMAN SERVICES	DEPARTMENT OF HOMELAND SECURITY	DEPARTMENT OF HOUSING AND URBAN DEVELOPMENT	DEPARTMENT OF THE INTERIOR	DEPARTMENT OF JUSTICE
DEPARTMENT OF LABOR	DEPARTMENT OF STATE	DEPARTMENT OF TRANSPORTATION	DEPARTMENT OF THE TREASURY	DEPARTMENT OF VETERANS AFFAIRS

Other Significant Reporting Entities

Environmental Protection Agency General Services Administration National Aeronautics and Space Administration National Science Foundation Office of Personnel Management Small Business Administration Social Security Administration US Agency for International Development	US Nuclear Regulatory Commission Defense Security Cooperation Agency Export-Import Bank of the United States Farm Credit System Insurance Corporation Federal Communications Commission Federal Deposit Insurance Corporation General Fund of the US Government Millennium Challenge Corporation	National Credit Union Administration Overseas Private Investment Corporation Pension Benefit Guaranty Corporation Railroad Retirement Board Securities and Exchange Commission Smithsonian Institution Tennessee Valley Authority US Postal Service

In Conservatorship

Fannie Mae   Freddie Mac

	SIGNIFICANT RELATED ENTITIES		
	The Federal Reserve	The Farm Credit System	
	Federal Home Loan Banks		

Graph entitles the US Government/the Constitution/branches and reporting entities.

Adapted from USA Facts.

PRESIDENT OBAMA'S EXECUTIVE ORDERS

After the Sandy Hook Incident

© Evan El-Amin/Shutterstock.com

On December 14, 2012, Adam Lanza woke up, shot his mother in their Newport, Connecticut home, then went to Sandy Hook Elementary School and proceeded to shoot 28 people, including himself.

The public outcry was understandably ferocious because this was just 1 of 30 mass killings in 2013. It has become the American norm to suspect that, at any given time, someone may walk into a school or a mall or a theatre and shoot as many people as possible before law enforcement is able to contain the situation.

Statistics have shown that there have been 74 school shootings since the Sandy Hook incident. It's safe to say that if there is a week in which school is in session, there is a good chance that there will also be at least one school shooting. There is a general mistrust of the government regarding gun control because, despite many politicians' best efforts, there are apparently more people making money in the government from the sale of firearms than there are people dying. As such, any bills, measures, and laws that oppose the distribution of guns to be akin to giving out candy during Halloween have been met with filibusters and have come to a halt in the Senate. While the media and politicians were in a frenzy over who was to blame for the Sandy Hook tragedy, how gun control was either too strict or too lenient, scapegoating music and video games, demonizing mental illness, and showing tearful parent interviews, there was a very pressing question that many urgently needed to be answered: What is the President going to do about the issue Americans have with mass murder, especially in schools?

In January 2013, President Obama launched a plan that included 23 measures that would affect how easily people are able to obtain military-grade assault rifles and other weapons. There are very few regulations on who can carry a firearm and what kind of weapon someone is allowed to carry. The President hoped that these new measures would require more thorough background checks, pass stronger bans on assault-grade weapons, limit the amount of ammunition that could be in a magazine, strengthen school emergency evacuation plans, eradicate armor-piercing ammunition from the streets, and ensure quality medical coverage for mental patients, particularly youth. All of these efforts would have been great steps forward in a problem that has only gotten worse in the last two decades since the Columbine shootings brought school shootings and mass murder to a new generation's radar.

However, the NRA has been particularly vocal in the criticism against such political changes, under the auspices of being concerned that denying people the right to carry military-grade weapons will somehow infringe on our Constitutional rights. The NRA has quite a bit of influence in politics and the media and has certainly moved the dialogue away from guns being dangerous in the wrong hands to how video games, music, and television are simply brainwashing children to use guns irresponsibly. Ultimately, Congress did not pass the measures, marking a particularly hard blow to President Obama's second term. Time will only tell how many more children will have to be shot before the government can make changes that will be effective in making schools, movie theatres, and other public locations safe without fear of a killing spree.

Executive Power, Immigration Enforcement, and Family Separations

Contributed by Michael Guzy

Introduction

As with many policy issues over the past century, immigration policy and enforcement has increasingly centered around the executive branch. Armed with the ability to control the vast bureaucratic machinery that guides immigration, the executive can usually avoid the typical checks that the other branches of government can utilize against executive expansion. This control has tightened to the extent that the other branches of government, as well as the public, can really do nothing but react to executive immigration policy—policy which has left a lot of damage in its wake. One particularly infamous example of such policy was the Trump Administration's April 2018 "Zero Tolerance Policy": a policy which many credit as the instigator of a systematic campaign of family separation on the Southwest United States Border. This article attempts to give an overview of the separation policy, from its implementation to the organizations involved, and attempt to situate this policy into a wider context of immigrant detention contemporaneously and historically. In the end, despite the policy eventually being defeated, we will see that very little ultimately has been done to stem the executive's hold over immigration throughout this controversy.

The Implementation of Family Separation

It must first be stated that the Trump Administration's family separation policy was percolating in our immigration system's administrative organs *far* before the "Zero Tolerance Policy" was enacted via memorandum. Various religious organizations were sounding the alarm around increased cases of separated children as far back as the May of *2017* (Al Otro Lado et al., 2017) and the very judicial case that demanded the reunification of the families, *Ms. L., et al v. U.S. Immigration and Customs Enforcement ("ICE")*, began in 2017. From this, any sort of analysis of the memorandum must be made with the consideration that it did very little to actually change what was occurring on the ground already, besides perhaps mobilizing the policy more systematically. The memorandum does, however, provide us with some information around the underlying logic of the separations.

The memorandum never specifically states anything relating to family separations. Instead, it states there will be a "Zero Tolerance Policy" for offenses under 8 U.S.C. § 1325(a), which "prohibits both attempted illegal entry and illegal entry into the United States by an alien" (U.S. Department of Justice, 2018). Essentially, the memorandum criminalized all attempts to cross the Southwest United States Border without documentation. This created the (intended or unintended) side-effect of fathers and mothers crossing the border with immigrant children becoming criminals. Under the Flores Settlement—which outlined protections to undocumented immigrant children, and further 2015 updates to that settlement, the Department of Homeland Security (DHS)—the government organization that implements immigration policy—"must release children to an appropriate adult or transfer them to a non-secure, licensed facility within three to five days of apprehension" (Human Rights First, 2018). Suddenly, with the implementation of the Zero Tolerance Policy, many immigrant children had no "appropriate adults" to be released to, as their parents were criminals.

Thus, the separated families were sent into the immigrant detention machinery of the DHS. The parents, after spending time in Customs and Border Protection (CBP) holding facilities, typically near the border, got shipped to ICE detainment facilities—facilities usually contracted out by for-profit prison companies; the children, after also spending time separated in CBP facilities, got shipped as "unaccompanied minors" to Office of Refugee Resettlement facilities—facilities typically contracted out by nonprofit organizations. These facilities were ill-equipped to handle these new sorts of detainees, immigrant families could not contact each other easily, and many children could not be found or identified in the chaos.

A Brief History of Immigration Enforcement

All of these events should be alarming by themselves, but they carry on new, more dire meanings when one analyzes these separations in the context to the executive's historical control over immigration. Legislation around immigrants has always carried on a certain racialized character, more obvious in the past and more obscured in the present, and this racialization has often collided with executive power in very concerning ways.

The first set of restrictive federal immigration laws, the Chinese Exclusion Act of 1882, and its subsequent iterations were primarily the act of Congress, and its first iteration was actually vetoed in 1878 by then-president Rutherford B. Hayes. These Acts initiated further explicitly racialized immigration laws for decades to come. Such racial prerequisites were replaced by a restrictive quota system in the 1952 Immigration Acts, and discrimination based on race was removed entirely in the 1965 Immigration and Nationality Act. As it happens, as the language around immigration became softer and subtler legislatively, the executive has had significantly more control over the process of immigration.

Adam Cox and Cristina Rodriguez outline this shift in control throughout their legal-historical work around United States Immigration policy. Though Congress has continually "maintained control over the formal legal governing" immigrants (2009, p. 483), the executive branch has an extensive ability to "screen" immigrants (p. 497), allowing the executive branch to decide the ultimate status of immigrants. Through these screening practices, the executive branch has been able to continuously subvert the "neutral" aims of Congressional immigration law by deciding on immigrant groups to keep in and immigrant groups to keep out.

This sometimes can result in very contradictory policy making based on the changing political currents of the times. For example, while during the 1970s the presidency used large-scale parole powers to temporarily let in immigrants from Haiti, Cuba, and other countries, much to the aggrievement of Congress (p. 503), during the 1981 Haitian refugee crisis President Reagan proclaimed that undocumented Haitians "threatened the welfare and safety of communities in South Florida" allowing them to be interdicted without impunity (High Seas Interdiction of Illegal Aliens, 1981). Contradictory or not, this shows that though Congress might write the law around immigration, the president ultimately controls the strings.

Implications

The sort of language used by Reagan is repeated throughout the in general justifications of the "Zero Tolerance Policy," painting the border as "the front lines of [a] battle" (Sessions, 2018) and immigrants a "challenge to…public safety, national security, and the rule of law" (U.S. Department of

Justice, 2018). Of course, such rationalizations barely obscure the highly racialized nature of this policy, as it consisted *only* of the Southwest border, a border which is crossed overwhelmingly by Latin-Americans. The implied connection that Sessions wants us to make is that Latin-Americans are dangerous threats to public safety and national security, much in the same way that the Chinese and Haitians were supposedly "threats" to the nation.

What is even more concerning is how this policy grafts onto the general trajectory of immigration policy as it relates to the executive. These separations were done with essentially *no* apparent policy, just implied policy, and even with that, the implied policy was not even what started the separations in the first place. This marks a concerning escalation of executive powers, as it means that large parts of our immigration system were independently separating families on their own volition without any apparent orders to do so for nearly a year, and without any sort of public acknowledgement, media attention, or political accountability. It is a disturbing and dangerous sign to see something so violating and extreme occurring under no scrutiny for so long. Consider, briefly, the Chinese Exclusion Acts versus immigration policy now, the former acts were racist and brutal, but they were out in the open, challengeable; now, with immigration policy sealed within the functions of the executive branch, such lines are often obscured, and often concern a variety of organizations that make holistically challenging policy difficult.

Conclusion

Ultimately, it was the chaotic implementation of the separations that ultimately defeated the separation policy. The procedures simply were too ad-hoc and poorly thought out to be considered admissible by the court in the *Ms. L.* case (2018, pp. 1144–1145). Almost concurrent to that decision, the Trump Administration sent out Executive Order 13841 (2018) which effectively ended the separation policy. It was the power of the public that helped these victories along, but the public is a very fickle and forgetful body. These victories, though important, were rather limited in terms of the greater battle to stave off executive power, especially concerning immigration. The greater regime of immigrant detention still grinds on, barely implicated throughout this process. The court battle around the case, though it reached an important decision, never questioned the general *ethics* of children in detention, just the general process in which it occurred in this instance. If anything, this development might simply cause changes to the Flores Settlement which would instate *family* detention centers instead of separate detention centers. Essentially, never in this controversy did the executive ever lose the general initiative around immigration policy; in the end, other forces could only react, just like they did at the start, as President Trump signed the order to end the separations.

REFERENCES

Al Otro Lado et al. (2017). *RE: The separation of family members apprehended by or found inadmissible while in U.S. Customs and Border Protection (CBP) custody at the U.S.–Mexico Border* [Email Document]. Retrieved from the Women's Refugee Commission website: https://www.womensrefu geecommission.org/images/zdocs/Family-Separation-Complaint-FINAL-PUBLIC-12-11-17.pdf

Cox, A. B., & Rodriguez, C. M. (2009). The president and immigration law. *Yale Law Journal, 119*(3), 458–547. Retrieved from Yale Digital Law Commons website: https://digitalcommons.law.yale.edu/ylj/vol119/iss3/2/

High Seas Interdiction of Illegal Aliens. (1981). *Proclamation No. 4865. 3 C.F.R. 50* [Web Page]. Retrieved from National Archives website: https://www.archives.gov/federal-register/codification/proclamations/04865.html

Human Rights First. (2018). *The flores settlement and family incarceration: A brief history and next steps* [Web Document]. Retrieved from Human Rights First website: https://www.humanrightsfirst.org/sites/default/files/FLORES_SETTLEMENT_AGREEMENT.pdf

Ms. L. v. U.S. Immigration and Customs Enforcement, 310 F. Supp. 3d 1133. (S.D. Cal. 2018). Retrieved from Case Text website: https://casetext.com/case/ms-l-v-us-immigration-customs-enforcement

Sessions, J. (2018, April 6). *Memorandum for federal prosecutors along the southwest border* [Memorandum]. Retrieved from The U.S. Office of the Attorney General website: https://www.justice.gov/opa/press-release/file/1049751/download

U.S. Department of Justice. (2018). *Attorney general announces zero-tolerance policy for criminal illegal entry* [Web Page]. Retrieved from the U.S. Department of Justice website: https://www.justice.gov/opa/pr/attorney-general-announces-zero-tolerance-policy-criminal-illegal-entry

CHAPTER TEN

Supreme Justice: U.S. Courts and Constitutional Rights

© Jack R Perry/Shutterstock .com

In this section, we will explore how the Supreme Court affects laws through their opinions and rulings. We will examine how the diversity of decisions made by the judicial branch have impacted communities nationwide. Lastly, we will look at how we can better utilize the courts to make more necessary changes in America.

© Tinnaporn Sathapornnanont/Shutterstock .com

The Supreme Court is responsible for trying appellate cases that have already gone through lower courts and cases between states or high-ranking ministers, such as ambassadors. Most of the cases that the Supreme Court tries are appeals for previous cases. Throughout history, the Supreme Court has handed down opinions for major cases that eventually played a role in passing groundbreaking laws. Important cases that you may be familiar with include *Pace v. Alabama* (1883), *Loving v. Virginia* (1967), *Plessy v. Ferguson* (1896), and *Brown v. Board of Education* (1954). Before the *Pace v. Alabama* case, African Americans and white citizens were unable to marry. It was termed miscegenation and deemed highly inappropriate because it violated the Virginia Racial Integrity Act. The *Pace v. Alabama* case marks the first time that this rule was challenged and, although it was ultimately upheld in law, it laid the groundwork for the *Loving v. Virginia*, case that made it legal nationwide for African Americans and white people to marry.

How the Supreme Court Works

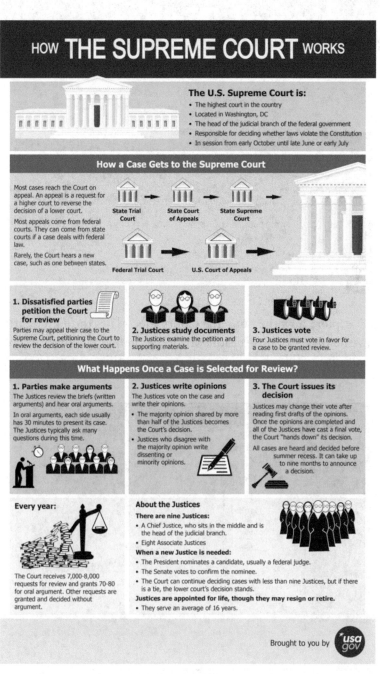

The *Plessy v. Ferguson* case coined the "separate but equal" phrase and is one of the many examples of institutionalized racism that became commonplace in America. The *Brown v. Board of Education* ruling found that separate did not mean equal and that, if there should be equal facilities, then those facilities should be utilized by anyone who would like to take advantage of them. These examples have only applied to a few racially motivated cases; there are still many cases regarding women, immigration, LGBTQIA issues, and workers' rights which are considered revolutionary in their rulings but are also still being held up because of an outdated agenda that is meant to uphold a white, patriarchal, and cisgender-centric tradition in America. Though there have been many strides in the Supreme Court and how they pass down opinions, there is still much to be done before Americans can consider itself a fair or equal country to all citizens.

One predominant reason for the slow progress toward change and social evolution is the tradition that Supreme Court Justices be white, older men. As such, there has been a major push toward maintaining the status quo concerning rights and privileges that American citizens should find attainable on the basis of the amount of work that someone puts into it. The status quo has worked in favor of the elite who have the power to influence how laws are shaped and who ends up on the Supreme Court bench.

That is why it was such a revolutionary decision to have Justice Thurgood Marshall become the first African American Supreme Court Justice in 1967, which was incidentally the same year that the *Loving v. Virginia* opinion came through; why Justice Sandra Day O'Connor was a feminist pioneer in 1981 for being the first female Justice; and why Justice Sonia Sotomayor becoming the first Latina woman in August 2009 was both a great step for feminism, women of color, and people of color, and also telling about the American system that this finally happened in the 21st century. It is still subversive for people of color to be on the Supreme Court bench, garnering quite a bit of media buzz as though this behavior merits reward. Despite the fact that there are various ideological beliefs in the Supreme Court, this branch of government has proven to be the most radically inclusive and has made it possible for much-needed change to happen in America. However, this does not mean that the disenfranchised and underrepresented have an ally yet. It means that there is an opportunity to finally have a more diverse set of voices heard and make important changes through the Supreme Court's legality.

JUSTICE SONIA SOTOMAYOR

Born in 1954, Sonia Sotomayor grew up in the South Bronx of New York City with her Puerto Rican family, who moved to New York to raise their children. When her father died when she was just 9-year old, her mother had to make her wages as a nurse at a methadone clinic work for her two children. As such, she taught her children that education was important, often driving them around to look at the colleges in their area and saying that they would be going to those colleges eventually.

With this as her background, Justice Sotomayor was a stellar student at Princeton University for undergraduate school and Yale Law School for her J.D. She worked with her Puerto Rican community for many years before being selected to be a Justice.

Justice Sonia Sotomayor was elected as a Justice of the Supreme Court in August 2009, becoming the first Latina woman to be elected to the Supreme Court. She has come to embody the "American Dream" being possible, a piece of rhetoric that has been used in the United States since the country was founded but seems wholly unattainable except for a select few.

The media coverage surrounding Justice Sotomayor's selection to be an Associate Justice bordered on exotification in some ways, while there was quite a bit of criticism of her liberal viewpoints, as though those liberal opinions were not shaped on her fully human experience as an American who has seen the world through the lens of being a Puerto Rican woman. In downgrading the viewpoints or focusing on her being the first Latina in the Supreme Court, it makes it easier for the public to dismiss her ideas in many ways because they are focused on how she is different from the rest of the Justices, as though that is a bad character trait. Throughout her career, she has proven to be a competent attorney and judge and, though one may not necessarily agree with all of her rulings or politics, her role is still one that should be respected, more than her race, her gender, or her particular political affiliation or philosophies.

However, despite the media still being unable to know how to represent people of color, specifically women of color, when something monumental happens that is not to detract from Justice Sotomayor's journey and her great accomplishment. She offers a unique perspective on a majority-white male bench in the Supreme Court, a perspective that is deeply necessary, given the many cases that go through the Supreme Court that often involve people of color and women. Because of her background, coming from a modest childhood and working with the Puerto Rican community, she actually knows how people live and what their daily struggles look like, making her more able to make a sympathetic decision regarding cases that could eventually affect a large amount of people. Justice Sotomayor is certainly a step in the right direction in terms of seeing women of color in a position of power and influence, which means that women of color may also see some level of equality and fairness, a relatively invisible issue in the feminist movement.

THE SUPREME COURT'S SHAME: HIRABAYASHI, KOREMATSU, AND INTERNMENT

Contributed by Michael Guzy

Introduction

While very much part-and-parcel of the United States political system, the Supreme Court—and the judicial branch more broadly—enjoys an image of distance and insularity from the other branches of government. This image is somewhat backed-up by reality, the concerns and motives of Supreme Court Justices align to a different set of standards than other politicians, rather than legislate and make policy, or execute policy, the Supreme Court Judges policy based on the standards of one document—the Constitution. In this sense, the Supreme Court is a *reactionary* body, it can only react to what is already occurring in the other branches or in the United States at large. These facts allow the court to enjoy a degree of independence from standard "politics." This careful distance, however, can easily be shattered. In times of national crisis, when "political" questions arise which put the federal government at ends with the Constitution in very dramatic manners, the inherently political and limited powers of the Supreme Court can be shown in full focus. These limitations were never seen in a starker light than the infamous cases which dealt with Japanese internment during the Second World War (WWII), *Hirabayashi v. United States* and *Korematsu v. United States*.

Hirabayashi and Korematsu

The two cases come from the same overall process surrounding internment, after the attack on Pearl Harbor, a slew of executive orders and Congressional legislation allowed the creation of specific military districts in the United States headed by assigned generals. The assigned general of the Western District, General DeWitt, began instating policies directly targeting people of Japanese descent, including a mandatory curfew and—subsequently—an exclusion order which brought those same individuals into Civil Control Stations. These events marked the beginning of Japanese internment during WWII.

In the face of a massive military apparatus—sanctioned by both the executive branch and the legislative branch—arbitrarily invoking racial mandates on populations, the Supreme Court buckled. Though Hirabayashi was charged with two crimes, failing to obey the curfew order, and failing to report to a civil control station, the Hirabayashi case was only in response to Hirabayashi failing to obey the curfew order as the sentences were "ordered to run concurrently," (*Hirabayashi v. United States, 1943*, p. 81). This is an explicit narrowing of the case as the Supreme Court, by their own terms, refused to utilize the Fifth Amendment argument on both aspects of the case, despite the fact that the other process, also linked to internment, was different in scope and intensity than the curfew order. This quick omission is all the more egregious and flagrant based on the general arguments the Justices give justifying the curfew order. They maintained the fact that there is a certain qualified discretion that must be given to the military based on the circumstances of the war, and that a racialized curfew is within the limits of that discretion due to "national security." By conveniently *not* deciding on the constitutionality of the exclusion order, the Court bypassed making the decision on the more "intense" aspects of the case.

The Korematsu case was under almost the same set of circumstances, except that Korematsu was charged with violating the exclusion order. Justice Black, in offering the decision, only decided on the basis of the exclusion order, not the subsequent interning of Japanese Americans. Even though he outright acknowledges the possibility of such camps, he, in relation to the decision, emphatically states that "we are dealing with nothing but an exclusion order" (*Korematsu v. United States*, 1944, p. 223). Like the Hirabayashi case, the courts refused to go any further in how the military was conducting its orders. Also, like the Hirabayashi case, the court's decision revolved around the idea of national security allowing the revocation of certain constitutional privileges to groups of people like those of Japanese descent. From these two cases, it would seem that the Court deliberately ignored the context of these two situations as much as possible in order to allow the military to do whatever it wanted to the Japanese.

The Supreme Court's Dilemmas

These two cases are rather infamous examples of ineffectual legal work sanctioning downright shameful policy. These cases, shameful as they are to the reputation of the Supreme Court, show, rather intensely, the inherent structural and political limitations of the Supreme Court. The political realities of their decisions were never the starker; these cases were done when the strength of the government in the domestic sphere was at its absolute highest, with the military districting only a capstone to the militarization in light of WWII. Justice Douglass in the Hirabayashi decision stated the root of the problem outright in his concurrence, ruminating that "[Since] we cannot override the military judgement which lay behind these orders, it seems me necessary to concede that the army had the power to deal temporarily with these people on a group basis" (Hirabayashi, p. 106). This is a rather standout statement, as it concedes that the Supreme Court had functionally *no ability to stop* what was occurring even if they wanted to.

The Supreme Court was essentially in a lose–lose situation in this case, and ultimately decided to take the easy way out and simply abide by what the military was doing. The alternative option, deciding the cases for Hirabayashi and Korematsu, not only would have more than likely done nothing—as their decision probably would have been ignored—it might have also provoked a major intragovernmental crisis in the middle of the largest military conflict in the history of the world, which would have been a complete fiasco. Of course, such explanations for the Supreme Court's failure in this case neglect any personal anti-Japanese sentiment on part of the Justices. The rights of the Japanese might have been a "necessary" loss to in order to preserve national security for the Justices; or, in a more paternalizing manner, such orders might have been viewed as a way to "protect" Japanese Americans from a bloodthirsty public.

Other mechanisms related to the nature of the Supreme Court also had an impact in these judgments. The military orders the Supreme Court was deciding on were widespread, affected tens of thousands of Japanese Americans, and were already escalating by the time the Court got to them. Being the reactionary body it is, the Supreme Court had few ways to impact a fluid and escalating process, the infrastructure for internment was already there, and breaking that process would have been difficult. It also did itself few favors by the piecemeal manner in which it decided each exclusion order, as it made the possibility of retroactive justice toothless. What would it matter if the Supreme Court decided against curfew if the Japanese were already in internment camps? The narrowness of their decisions weakened them in another way; cases, naturally, take time, and war usually is a temporally restricted event (at least during WWII). Due to this, there would be no decision relating to the explicit internment of Japanese Americans because WWII ended before any case relating to internment got brought to the Supreme Court, by the Court's own refusal to decide on it. In a way, one of the Court's greatest assets in insulating them politically was also one of its greatest weaknesses in making an effective decision in these cases. Its insulation, ironically, exposed how fragile the Supreme Court is in moments like this.

Conclusion

In conclusion, the Korematsu and Hirabayashi cases expose the weaknesses of the Supreme Court when deciding cases based on national security. Ultimately, despite any supposed insulation or distance from the other powers-at-be, the Supreme Court is liable to the very same constraints and pressures as any other aspect of government. In some ways, it is also liable to different pressures and constraints than other branches. The *force of law* propping up the Court only really exists when the other branches accept that it exists, it has no enforcement mechanism that does their bidding besides pressure by the public. When that public is also compromised, the court is functionally dependent on the other branches for legitimacy. WWII saw the Court at its weakest, unable to detach itself from the rest of the government, the public, its functions, and its own biases. Thus, we have their support to let the military do whatever it wants to Japanese Americans. In this sense, these cases could be read as the Supreme Court protecting itself from its own shortcomings. By doing this, however, it sacrificed the rights and livelihoods of tens of thousands of Japanese Americans and the potential rights and livelihoods of *other* vulnerable ethnicities during wartime through its precedent. In retrospect, a decision against the government for these cases, no matter how futile it might have been in the short-term, would have been a principled and necessary stand on part of the Supreme Court against injustice, instead, it became complicit in that injustice.

IMPORTANT FACTS AND TERMS

Affirm: When the Supreme Court agrees with a lower court's decision after the case has gone through the appeals process.

Amicus curiae brief: From the Latin, "friend of the court," an amicus curiae brief is any information that is brought to the attention of the Supreme Court that may be helpful. This includes context for how the decision of the case may have a national effect on those not directly involved.

Appellate jurisdiction: The power of a court to hear appeal cases from lower courts, including modifying the previous court's ruling. The federal courts have jurisdiction over district courts and the Supreme Court has jurisdiction over federal courts.

Briefs: A summary of the important points of a case.

Charles River Bridge v. Warren Bridge: A 1785 Supreme Court case wherein the Charles River Bridge Company sued the legislature for violating their contract after hiring another company, the Warren Bridge Company, to build a second bridge near theirs, inevitably causing the Charles River Bridge to lose traffic. The Supreme Court held that the Charles River Bridge Company could not sue the legislature because the Charles River Bridge Company did not have rights over the water. As such, the legislature was free to contract with whoever they pleased to build a bridge over the river. Though the individual company saw an economic downturn, the public had more transportation options, which greatly improved infrastructure.

Civil law: A codified set of laws and statutes that are then applied to the case by the judge. The substantive law determines which acts are subject to criminal or civil prosecution, procedural law establishes if a particular act constitutes a criminal act, and penal law refers to the penalty. The judge works within a previously decided framework of laws.

Common law: A series of statutes and laws, that are not codified, that are based primarily on historical precedent. The presiding judge of any given case decides which precedents will apply to the case, which is then tried before a jury of one's peers. The judge then determines the sentence based on the jury's verdict.

Confirmation hearing: A session by a committee or a grand jury wherein witnesses give their testimony.

Courts of appeals: A court that relieves the Supreme Court of the responsibility of hearing every appeals case. A decision given by the courts of appeals is final, unless the Supreme Court decides to review the case.

Criminal law: A division of law practice that involves trying cases wherein someone committed a crime that possibly endangered the public's safety or displayed dangerous conduct. Oftentimes, civil law will be conflated as criminal law to maximize the penalty against the defendant.

District courts: A group of federal trial courts that have the jurisdiction to hear any case, either criminal or civil. There are 94 district courts.

Judicial activism: The belief that Supreme Court Judges should interpret the Constitution in such a way as to make a difference and a change that will benefit the American public.

Judicial restraint: The belief that Supreme Court Judges should interpret the Constitution literally and exercise self-control to leave personal beliefs out of the ruling.

Judicial review: A function of the checks and balances/separation of powers system in the United States, the judicial branch has the authority to review and possibly override any action by the executive and legislative branches, according to the Constitution.

Judiciary Act of 1789: Signed into law by former President George Washington, the Judiciary Act of 1789 established the federal court system, including the Supreme Court and allowing the Congress to establish lower federal courts as they deemed necessary.

Justiciability: A matter that the federal courts can rightfully try. In order for a case to be justiciable, the plaintiff must be standing, the court must not be advising, and the issue must be cogent to a larger framework.

Oral argument: A lawyer's opportunity to summarize their position on the case before the court and to answer the judge's questions regarding the case.

Original jurisdiction: A court's authority to hear a case before appellate review.

Pardon: Crime forgiveness that is often granted by the Governor of a state, but can also be granted by the President.

Precedent: A judicial decision that may be used as an example or legal standard for subsequently similar cases.

Remand: To send back. Legally speaking, a federal court can send a case back to the lower court if they have made a decision that the lower court needs to act on.

Reprieve: To delay a criminal's sentence or punishment, often when a pardon is possible or when the case is being otherwise reviewed for another reason.

Reverse: To overthrow, invalidate, or repeal. The Supreme Court can reverse the decision of a lower court.

Rule of four: In order for certiorari to be granted, four Supreme Court Justices must vote in favor of the grant.

Stare decisis: From the Latin, "let the decision stand," stare decisis is the policy of the court to stand by a previous court ruling regarding a case. See "precedent."

Supreme Court: The judicial branch of government that tries high-ranking cases and, normally, appeal cases that have a national effect. Often, the Supreme Court's decisions become amendments or affect laws.

Writ of certiorari: A writ issued by an appellate court to a lower court, directing the lower court to send the case record for review. A writ of certiorari is how the Supreme Court hears most of its cases.

REFERENCES

Black, H. L., & Supreme Court of the United States. (1944). *U.S. Reports: Korematsu v. United States, 323 U.S. 214* [Periodical]. Retrieved from the Library of Congress website: https://www.loc.gov/item/usrep323214/